SUBTIDAL
GALAPAGOS

A colony of orange tube corals
(*Tubastraea* sp), their appendages
stretched out in a constant search
for food, adds an explosion of
colour to the subtidal world of the
Galápagos.

SUBTIDAL
GALAPAGOS

EXPLORING THE WATERS OF DARWIN'S ISLANDS

BY JAMES CRIBB   CAMDEN HOUSE

Canadian Cataloguing in Publication Data

Cribb, James, 1956-
   Subtidal Galápagos

Includes index.
ISBN 0-920656-47-1

1. Marine biology - Galápagos Islands - Pictorial works. 2. Galápagos Islands - Description and travel - Views. I. Title.

QH198.G3C75   1986   574.9866'5   C86-094429-8

Trade distribution by
Firefly Books
3520 Pharmacy Avenue, Unit 1-C
Scarborough, Ontario
Canada M1W 2T8

Camden House Publishing Ltd.
7 Queen Victoria Road
Camden East, Ontario K0K 1J0

Species Identification
The author has endeavoured to include in the photograph captions the scientific names of as many of his subjects as possible. However, the precise identification of marine life is such that this is not always feasible without laboratory dissection. Thus some captions include only the genus names, and others with dozens of similar species, such as sponges, anemones and corals, are identified only by their common names.

To Andrea, without whom this book might never have been completed.

A group of sedentary polychaetes, distant marine cousins of the earthworm and leech, blankets the ocean floor in a beautiful pattern that belies their simple nature.

Acknowledgments

For an expedition that spanned so many miles and so many months, I am at a loss as to where to begin acknowledging the help I received along the way. I shall have to limit my expressions of gratitude to those whose assistance directly influenced the outcome of the project, with the hope that others who offered support will accept a global thanks.

Sr. Jaime Molina, Consul General of Ecuador, for arranging our visas in Toronto; Sr. Poncé, Director de Forrestal, for updating my permission to carry out our project in the Galápagos Islands; Sr. Miguel Cifuentes, Administrator, Galápagos National Park, for his guidance and permission to work in the islands; Judy Carvalhal, Fiddi, Karl, Fritz and Carmen Angermeyer, for sharing with us their intimate knowledge of these islands; Patricia and Jorgé Valdivieso, our open-hearted neighbours and owners of the *Normita*; my father-in-law, Des Clements, Toronto, for logistical support far beyond the call of familial duty; Tom Hirtz, Toronto, for equipment and technical assistance; Bob McBay, Victoria, for help with camera gear and film; Meredith Clements, for assisting with the considerable work preparing for and during our sojourn in the islands; Helen and Charles Hornby, Cumbaya, Ecuador, whose loving support sustained us during our stay.

To Jack Grove, who freely shared with me his encyclopaedic knowledge of the Galápagos marine life, who accurately identified my slides and whose comments and criticisms of the manuscript have led to a more factual and comprehensive rendering of subtidal Galápagos. I only wish that time and distance had not prevented him from working more closely with me on this book.

I am indebted to my guide Mario Possa for sharing with me his vast and enlightened understanding of the magical islands he calls home.

And finally, I must thank my wife, Andrea, for helping to realize a dream that has consumed us ever since we have been married and for being a companion during the most difficult and rewarding experiences I have known. This book is as much hers as it is mine.

A colony of gorgonian, or horny, corals seems more of a botanical fossil than a group of tiny animals clinging to one another. Common to shallow, warm waters, gorgonian colonies can branch out to a width of 10 feet.

Designed by
Linda J. Menyes

Colour separations by
Herzig Somerville Limited
Toronto, Ontario

Printed and bound in Canada by
D.W. Friesen & Sons Ltd.
Altona, Manitoba

Printed on 80-lb. Jensen Gloss

A blenny (*Ophioblennius steindachneri*), its doleful eyes watching my approach, pokes its head out of a rock scallop shell encrusted with coralline algae.

Contents

My dives in the Galápagos were
journeys into the unknown, a
world of exotic fish, rare coral
and mystical caverns seldom
visited by man.

Exploring Paradise

Diving the uncharted waters of a
mystical subtidal world

"Dolphins alongside!" The cry from the stern shattered my reverie. I snatched my camera and hurried toward the bow, squinting as I scanned the sea. The equatorial sun, though high above the horizon, had not yet reached its zenith above the Galápagos Islands; the intense rays bounced off the water like myriad glittering diamonds. I grabbed the headstay, leaned over the gunwale and found myself staring into the deep brown eye of a dolphin that was gliding effortlessly in the bow wave. Its eye shone with the innocence and curiosity of a newborn yet at the same time conveyed the understanding of a wise old seafarer. I was entranced. Then it was gone, with not a ripple left upon the water. Others came, perhaps 18 to 20, all vying for the cherished spot at the bow. I decided to join them in the water.

I called for the captain to cut our speed and for Mario Possa, my assistant, to pull alongside the Zodiac tender that was in tow. Jack Grove, a marine biologist who was accompanying me on this trip to the western islands, was already gathering his equipment as I went below to collect a couple of underwater cameras. In the interest of haste, I decided against putting on my rubber wet suit, despite the coolness of the waters that surround the Galápagos Islands; instead, I settled for a T-shirt to protect me from the coarse straps and backpack on my scuba tank. With our equipment in place, we jumped aboard the inflatable Zodiac and raced ahead of the *Normita*, the 32-foot fishing boat I had chartered for the trip.

The largest group of dolphins lay slightly off to starboard. As we approached, they circled and began crisscrossing only inches in front of the inflatable, sometimes making spectacular leaps out of the water. I fumbled with my face mask, excited at the prospect of swimming with such a playful pod. As Mario stopped the engine, Jack and I rolled overboard.

It took a moment to become oriented after the shock of hitting 68-degree (F) water. As I attempted to gain my bearings, I could hear the high-pitched squeaks of the dolphins as they communicated with each other. As they came nearer, the intensity of their shrieks increased, and I could feel the pressure waves that carried their cries through the water. By then, there were 8 to 10 dolphins swimming around us. I was hoping they would venture closer, because the murkiness of the water hampered my ability to take clear photographs. Still, I was delighted with their performance, an inspiring display of aquatic antics that seemed to be acted out for the sheer joy of it.

The Galápagos archipelago is unusual because of its location at the juncture of several different currents and wind systems, some cold, others warm. This Moorish idol (*Zanclus cornutus*), an Indo-Pacific species, clings to its warm-water heritage in the northern regions where the waters are subtropical.

After several minutes, the dolphins disappeared, leaving us hovering alone in the water. I had taken few pictures because of the poor visibility but was grateful for the chance to swim with the dolphins. Nearby, a shadow passed, then disappeared. Hoping for more dolphins, I checked my camera and strobe settings and surveyed the water about me. Seconds later, the shadow reappeared, but I sensed it was not a dolphin. The fluid, animated movements were gone, replaced by the spasmodic drive of a frenzied shark. Alerted by the dolphins' activity, a six-foot black-tip shark commanded the now vacant arena. But rather than finding the spoils of the dolphins' feeding, it had come upon me, an alien creature.

Hurtling forward, the shark jerked from side to side as if unable to choose its direction. Its cold, unblinking eyes regarded me from less than 12 feet away. The image of the friendly dolphins off the bow of the *Normita* seemed an eternity away, though, in fact, only 15 minutes had passed since they had approached us. For the first time in 10 years of diving, I felt raw fear. I was in open sea in the shark's domain, vulnerable, defenceless.

I thought back to the night several months earlier when, in the comfort of an easy chair in my home in Ontario, I had decided to strike a "shark billy" from my list of equipment needs. Funds for the Galápagos project were running low, and I had foreseen difficulties in transporting a firearm into a South American country. It had seemed like a sound decision at the time.

Now, there was nothing I could do but hold my camera housing at arm's length in a futile attempt to protect myself. I glanced quickly upward in search of the Zodiac but remembered that I had instructed Mario to keep the boat at a distance. The shark continued its erratic advance, now seven, maybe six, feet away. Suddenly, it arched its back, the sleek body convulsed from nose to tail, and then it was gone.

I exhaled slowly, releasing the air that had grown stale from holding my breath. I was shaken but, luckily, unharmed: the shark had merely warned me away. I ascended, gathering my thoughts after a harrowing encounter with one of the sea's most feared inhabitants. Just before I surfaced, I heard the dolphins conversing in the distance.

My heart was still pounding as Mario helped me into the Zodiac. It felt good to be topside, and I took deep breaths of

Disturbed by my approach, a three-foot-wide stingray (*Urotrygon* sp) erupts from the sand and flees. I moved away quickly, as the venomous spine at the base of its whiplike tail can deliver a painful cut.

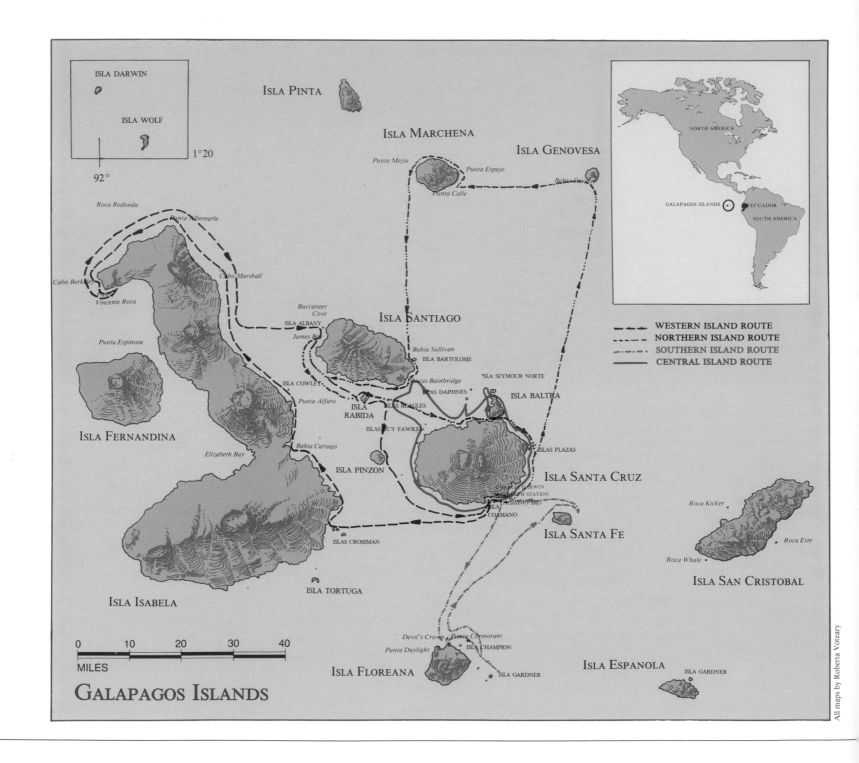

ISLA DARWIN

ISLA WOLF

1°20

92°

ISLA PINTA

ISLA MARCHENA

ISLA GENOVESA

Punta Mejia   *Punta Espejo*

Punta Calle   *Bahia Darwin*

NORTH AMERICA

GALAPAGOS ISLANDS   ECUADOR

SOUTH AMERICA

Roca Redonda

Punta Albemarle

Cabo Marshall

Cabo Berkeley

Punta Vincente Roca

Buccaneer Cove

ISLA SANTIAGO

ISLA ALBANY

James Bay

Punta Espinosa

Bahia Sullivan

ISLA BARTOLOME

ISLA SEYMOUR NORTE

WESTERN ISLAND ROUTE

NORTHERN ISLAND ROUTE

SOUTHERN ISLAND ROUTE

CENTRAL ISLAND ROUTE

ISLA COWLEY   *Islas Bainbridge*

Islas Daphnes   ISLA BALTRA

Punta Alfaro   ISLA RABIDA   *Islas Beagles*

ISLA FERNANDINA   *Islas Guy Fawkes*

Elizabeth Bay   *Bahia Cartago*   ISLAS PLAZAS

ISLA PINZON   ISLA SANTA CRUZ

Estación Darwin Research Station

Academy Bay

ISLA COAMANO

ISLAS CROSSMAN   ISLA SANTA FE   *Roca Kicker*

Roca Este

ISLA ISABELA   ISLA TORTUGA   *Roca Whale*

ISLA SAN CRISTOBAL

0   10   20   30   40

MILES

Devil's Crown   *Punta Cormorant*

Punta Daylight   ISLA CHAMPION

ISLA FLOREANA   ISLA GARDNER   ISLA ESPANOLA   ISLA GARDNER

GALAPAGOS ISLANDS

All maps by Roberta Voteary

the warm, sweet tropical air. Jack was already safely aboard the inflatable. He had enjoyed the dolphins but had not seen the shark.

As we excitedly compared our dives, Mario pointed out that the dolphins were still dancing attendance a hundred feet away. Convinced that I had not captured good photographs of them, I decided to rejoin them. Jack had equipment problems that forced him to stay aboard.

Mario raced the Zodiac toward the pod, and soon the dolphins were riding the bow wave. From my position atop the starboard pontoon, I could almost touch the dolphins as they vaulted through the air. Mario cut the engine, and I eased into the water. While descending, I caught myself nervously scanning my surroundings. Close encounters, even harmless ones, fade slowly from memory.

The dolphins, however, were behaving marvellously, and before long, I was engrossed in their magical performance. They seemed more relaxed this time, swimming leisurely within camera range. I was nearing the end of my roll of film when I was hit from behind, the impact snapping my head back and knocking it against the tank valve. Stunned, I twisted around in time to see a high-pointed caudal fin disappearing into the hazy water. I had been "bumped" by a shark — possibly the same one that only minutes earlier had warned me off. It was time to leave the water.

I finned hurriedly back to the Zodiac and heaved my tank, weight belt and camera gear to Mario, keeping a wary eye on the water beneath me. When I hauled myself into the safety of the inflatable and explained my sudden return, Jack informed me that a shark bumps its prey to determine edibility, and it does so with its mouth open. If such is the case, this one must have hit my tank, because I was unmarked.

The dolphins were now several hundred feet away, but even if they had been closer, I doubt that I could have forced myself to dive again. It is a peculiar sensation to be the victim of an animal's attack, and I needed some time to digest the experience.

While my first meeting with a shark was one of the most dramatic events of five months of diving throughout the isolated Galápagos Islands, it also clearly reflected the dichotomous nature of the area. The Galápagos are a storehouse of landscapes and creatures that offer a much-needed counterpart to the technological complexity of our world. In the islands, few buffers exist to soften the reality of nature. When the dolphin

plays, its merriment is pure; when the shark hunts, it stalks to kill.

My work took me from the southern shores of Isla Floreana to the northern reaches of Isla Genovesa, from Isla San Cristóbal in the east to Isla Fernandina in the west. The area I visited along the way included 16 islands and several islets and rocky outcroppings spread over about 18,000 square miles — an area about half the size of Iceland — where the marine life has been shaped by ocean currents into four distinct marine provinces.

I found an extraordinary collection of marine creatures that by rights simply do not belong together. A striking example of this confronted me in the channel between Isla Santiago and the circular island of Sombrero Chino. I passed fluorescent green-and-yellow parrotfish feeding on tropical corals on my way to photograph Galápagos penguins flapping about on the jet-black lava at the water's edge. The Galápagos Islands — where the tropical meets the antarctic — are not limited to one or two such anomalies; they are made of them.

It was these peculiarities and the fact that approximately 23 percent of the undersea life comprises endemic species, animals found nowhere else but in the Galápagos, that attracted me.

Climbing into my cold-water wet suit under the equatorial sun was often a miserably hot experience best relieved by a leap into the icy waters.

Panamic-fanged blennies
(*Ophioblennius steindachneri*),
with their comic bug-eyed stare,
are one of 363 known species of
fish that inhabit the inshore
waters. They are commonly found
in crevices and cracks.

Despite the attention lavished upon the terrestrial wildlife of this archipelago, surprisingly little research has been conducted on the animals and plants that live below the tide line. As a photographer and chronicler of the earth's marine communities, I believed that the Galápagos offered me an unrivalled opportunity to explore virgin underwater retreats. What I saw was infinitely more impressive than what I had expected in even my most optimistic dreams.

During my five-month sojourn in the Galápagos, I swam with whales; was ringed by a school of hammerhead sharks (some 15 to 16 feet in length); observed marine iguanas taking to the sea for food; drifted in the currents with giant black-and-white manta rays; confronted a tiger shark in the open sea; stumbled across a patch of garden eels; and marvelled at the vivid hues of sea anemones and tunicates against a backdrop of black lava. I happened across a species of damselfish (*Nexilosus latifrons*) thought to have disappeared from the Galápagos during the devastating El Niño weather disturbance of 1982-83, and I took the first known photograph of the muppet-faced zebra moray eel (*Echidna zebra*) in southern Galápagos waters.

Occasionally, however, I came across scenes that left my gut in a knot: swatches of submarine landscapes laid bare by coral hunters; fishing boats at anchor, their decks crowded with rust-stained freezers where thousands of spiny lobsters awaited shipment to the mainland; expanses of empty sea bereft of the all-important food fish that are key links in the food chain of the submarine world. Clearly, humanity has left its unmistakable mark.

The marine community of the Galápagos Islands is without equal in the world, yet unlike its terrestrial counterpart, it remained unprotected, prey to anyone who wished to violate the laws of common-sense harvesting. The scars I saw in the underwater world were a frightening testimony to its frailty and, distressingly, to what could be its future.

The demise of the Galápagos marine life, however, would not come simply as a consequence of the local fishermen or coral hunters sallying forth daily from their tin-roofed huts in search of a modest living. The blame would also fall on our ignorance and neglect of a unique part of our natural heritage.

In the hope that a glimpse of this rare and astonishing submarine world might stir the hearts of people around the world, and in the belief that humanity will not willfully allow such a wondrous natural treasure to disappear, I present this book.

Tui A. De Roy/Bruce Coleman Inc.

Having spent the afternoon basking in the sun, a marine iguana (*Amblyrhynchus cristatus*), the Galápagos' most famous resident species, makes its way to the water to feed on lush beds of algae.

Diving Alone

The day dawned as it always does during May in the Galápagos Islands: one minute it was dark and the next minute the sun suddenly popped into the eastern sky — impatient, it seemed, to get on with the business of the day. Behind our rambling lava-rock bungalow, a sea lion splashed through the mangroves, while an orchestra of finches and mockingbirds performed a fine symphonic arrangement. My wife Andrea and I lay in bed quietly, not wishing to disturb the rehearsal.

A few hours later, I was aboard the *Normita*, a relic with more character than speed, chugging out of Academy Bay with the requisite bunch of bananas that all skippers have lashed to the stern cabin, a dietary hedge against uncertain rations of fresh fish and overpriced canned food. A moderately heavy surf ran beneath the keel, rocking us up and down before rushing on to dash its full force against the coastal bluffs, sending shafts of cold spray skyward. The steady drone of the diesel engine and the motion of the boat gave rise to the tranquillity of being at sea.

The captain was a thin old man with deep lines etched into his face. For 17 years, he had been weighing anchor and watching the village of Puerto Ayora disappear in his wake. Juan, his son, was along as cook, and my neighbour (and new owner of the *Normita*) Jorgé Valdivieso was there to supervise. Our destination was the central region of the Galápagos archipelago, where several islets and rocky outcroppings cluster around the two main islands of Santa Cruz and Santiago.

We steamed in an easterly direction from Puerto Ayora and, after passing the lava cliffs that mark the end of Academy Bay, proceeded north up the east coast of Isla Santa Cruz. Along the way, I spotted two hammerhead sharks swimming and a huge manta ray feeding just below the surface, its giant wings rhythmically propelling it forward. We approached to within 20 feet before the manta dived, with surprising speed, for the protection of deeper water. Floating on the surface was a raft of what appeared to be golden Frisbees which, as we moved closer, proved to be a school of 15 to 20 golden rays. Frigate birds soared tirelessly overhead, and boobies plummeted into the sea chasing baitfish.

The flat, monotonous coastline of eastern Isla Santa Cruz was our constant companion off the port side. Daily, the severe equatorial sun beats upon the black lava, and temperatures soar over 95 degrees F; only the hardiest of succulent plants survive. It was not a place where I would fancy being shipwrecked.

Two and a half hours after leaving Puerto Ayora, the *Normita*'s

Propelled forward by hundreds of tiny tubular feet, an orange nubbly sea star (*Oreaster occidentalis*) slowly scales a barnacle-covered rock. It bypasses the multitude of crustaceans around it in search of larger prey.

ancient engine dropped to an idle as we rounded the westernmost of a grouping of three islets called Rocas Gordon, near the popular tourist site of Islas Plazas. The three rocks jut out of the sea, their flanks forming steep cliffs where boobies nest by the hundreds and splotches of their guano, bleached white by the sun, contrast with the coal-black lava. The southern seas pass through the shallow channel between two of the islets, producing eddies that spew white foam. Between the onslaughts of crashing surf, we could hear the throaty woodwind calls of blue-footed boobies high above us.

The captain found harbour on the lee side and maintained the *Normita* at a safe distance from the rocks. As Juan and Jorgé transferred my scuba tank, weight belt and camera gear to the Zodiac, I tugged on my neoprene wet suit, perspiring in the fierce sun. It seemed ludicrous to be dressing so warmly at the equator, but without the insulation, I would not have been able to stay submerged in the chilly 68-degree water for any length of time.

Drenched in sweat, I leapt off the stern of the *Normita* into the sea to cool down before hauling myself aboard the Zodiac. Juan steered us close to the towering sheer wall near the northeast corner of the largest islet. Even on the sheltered side of the rock, the sea rose and fell five to six feet with each swell, tossing me to and fro as I tightened straps and rammed flippers onto my feet. Finally, armed and dressed for the sea, I rolled out of the Zodiac into the long-awaited waters of the Galápagos.

Thousands of tiny air bubbles swirled about me, racing for the surface. I swam through the effervescent mass to the face of the cliff and descended 20 feet to rest momentarily on a narrow ledge. I peered through the port of my camera housing to ensure that no water was seeping past the O-rings into my camera equipment. The focusing knob spun the ring that turned the lens; the aperture control clicked over the various f-stops; the film-advance lever wound a fresh frame in front of the shutter; and the shutter-release lever fired the camera and set off the strobe. I had verified all of these functions before entering the water, but it had become a ritual with me to repeat each operation once submerged. Because

The *Normita*, its deck loaded to capacity, was a functional, if painfully slow, craft. The shark lashed to its stern was caught inadvertently by biologist Jack Grove, who had been hoping for a meal-sized fish.

A sea squirt's siphons, used as
intakes and outtakes for food and
waste, protrude from a red
sponge. Under certain temperature
and salinity conditions, the seabed
is covered with these vividly
coloured invertebrates.

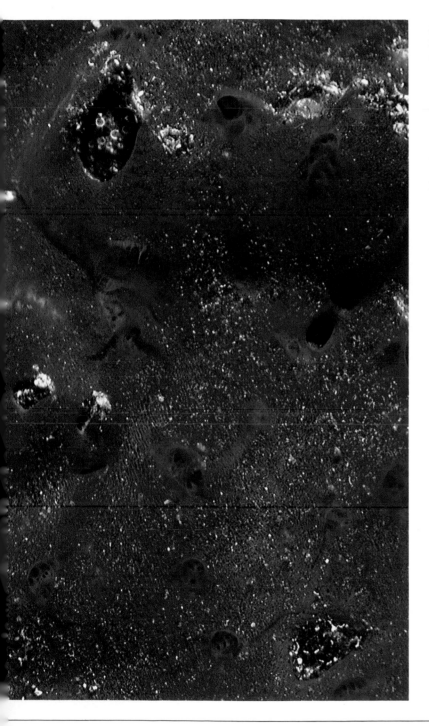

I have no access to the camera inside the housing while in the water, a simple problem such as a misaligned gear ring can result in an aborted dive.

My equipment in working order, I looked up to survey my surroundings. Hundreds of fish milled about me like bees around a hive. Shafts of sunlight plunged into the aquamarine ocean and scattered, striking one fish or another for a brief moment. In an animated display, the quivering mass sent countless flashes of colour through the water. Schools of jacks and yellow-finned tunas, whose sleek bodies and silver coloration allow them to blend in with their normal habitat of the open sea, formed a lustrous background. The yellows of butterflyfish and sergeant majors harmonized with the blues of queen angelfish and the greens of parrotfish. A huge school of creolefish added a warm red touch. The locals call these basslets *gringo* fish because their undersides look sunburned.

It was a golden moment for me. I had spent months away from the sea preparing for a season in the Galápagos, and finally, I was back in the underwater milieu, revelling in an oasis of life few humans have ever seen. The arduous struggle with time, money and bureaucracies for the opportunity to explore this little-known wilderness suddenly seemed insignificant.

The circumstances that had led my family and me to the famed Galápagos Islands had their beginnings on a cool September evening on southern Vancouver Island, British Columbia. A

Relatively free of predators and thriving on the abundant supply of fish, the extremely agile Galápagos sea lions (*Zalophus californianus wollebaeki*) are omnipresent throughout the islands.

miserable west-coast wind whipped rain against our living room window. Andrea and I had wanted to travel and explore the marine environments around the globe, and snug in our home on that inclement night, we decided that the undersea and coastal life of the Galápagos was the most unusual and the least studied.

Almost four years passed before we realized our dream, and we waited months to receive permission from the Galápagos National Park Service to work and photograph extensively in the islands. During that time, Andrea furthered her career as an oceanographic research chemist, and two books of my marine-life photographs of the Pacific Northwest and the Caribbean were published. We moved to Woodstock, Ontario, in 1982, and our family doubled in size with the addition of Jessica in the spring of that year and Michaela 20 months later, in the fall of 1983.

Despite the delay, we left Canada for Ecuador with a sense of urgency. Only the land portion of the Galápagos Islands had been declared a nature preserve in 1959, and the government was now contemplating protection of the island waters in light of rapidly diminishing marine resources. Thirty years ago, it would have been an easy task, but an industry of fishing, catching lobster and harvesting coral had been firmly established in the meantime, and now, many inhabitants depended on the sea for their livelihoods.

Nevertheless, Ecuador's Galápagos National Park Service as well as the internationally funded Charles Darwin Research Station seemed committed to the formation of a marine preserve in the islands. Both bodies were supportive of my project, especially, as the station's director, Dr. Friedemann Köster, pointed out, because "the marine part of the Galápagos Islands is, without doubt, the least known of the archipelago. While there exists ample photographic documentation of the terrestrial flora and fauna, nothing comparable exists of the marine environment." An attractive portfolio of undersea photographs would illustrate the need for the creation of a marine park.

I arrived in the Ecuadorian port city of Guayaquil on March 19, 1984. Located adjacent to the floodplain of the Rio Guayas,

King angelfish (*Holocanthus passer*), usually seen in groups, are one of the few marine animals that eat sponges. They are somehow able to tolerate the glass spicules and noxious chemicals of such a diet.

this dirty, steamy metropolis of more than one million inhabitants is Ecuador's marine gateway. I spent that evening strolling the banks of the Guayas, a mighty river crowded with a mixture of rusted freighters and motorized dugout canoes. The Guayas is not unlike the Mississippi River, with its muddy waters and slow, meandering pace. Clumps of vegetation, floating like horticultural rafts, moved onward to the sea.

My plan was to leave in two days aboard the *MV Bucanero*, a 285-foot cruise ship that tours the Galápagos Islands. Gordon Tours, operator of the *Bucanero*, had agreed to transport my 1,800 pounds of equipment for a modest fee once I had cleared it through customs. I spent the next day and a half in a frustrating shuffle between the customs bureau, the freight office and a brokerage firm, making pitifully little progress. Then I met Hector Gonzales, customs broker par excellence. Gonzales knew exactly which officials to approach — with the appropriate amount of money folded neatly into my passport — and finally, my 17 crates were released. With only minutes to spare, I reached the dock where the *Bucanero* was in its final stages of preparation for departure.

Once aboard, I wandered to the stern to watch the city sprawl of Guayaquil disappear behind the dense vegetation that borders the river. The cement and tin shacks huddled on noisy streets gave way to thatch-roofed wooden shanties perched on stilts above the Rio Guayas. Long canoes travelled close to the shore, their wakes like skeins of geese against a muddy sky. A cool breeze blew off the water.

The Rio Guayas is not navigated easily because much of its sizable breadth is riddled with treacherous sandbars. Four hours of wending our way around the shoals brought us to the entrance of a broad basin where the river spills into the Pacific Ocean. After a cold winter in inland Canada, the sight of the sea was wonderfully refreshing. I stood on the deck filling my lungs to capacity with the salty air and watched the sun, a glowing orb on the distant horizon, dissolve into the sea.

The jet airplane tends to make modern-day travellers ignorant of distances. From Guayaquil, the regularly scheduled TAME flight to the Galápagos Islands takes 1 hour and 40 minutes. The *Bucanero*, steaming at 14 knots, covers the 600-mile trip in approximately 45 hours, giving its passengers time to appreciate the islands' isolation. It was during our second day out from port, as the ship's huge diesel engines drove us toward our destination, that I began to understand how incredible it was that the

25

Two children stroll toward home on the outskirts of Puerto Ayora, the largest of the Galápagos villages. Most of its residents depend on the archipelago's 15,000 to 20,000 annual visitors for their livelihoods.

Galápagos Islands were inhabited by any flora and fauna at all.

These islands are considered to be purely oceanic, in that they have never been connected to continental South America; therefore, any organism that reached them had to cross this wide, open stretch of water first. And while theories abound about birds, plant seeds and spores being carried by the wind across the ocean, many plant and animal species are believed to have reached the islands by rafting. Heavy rains would pound the mainland forests, forcing small rivulets of water to seek lower ground. Soon, these tiny streams joined and tumbled into the swelling rivers, until finally, the banks could no longer contain them. Chunks of soil, held together by an intricate mesh of roots, were torn from the ground and swept away with the swirling mass of water. Plants and animals clung tenaciously to these rafts, many of which succumbed to the tremendous forces and broke apart, sinking to the river bottom.

Yet there were some rafts whose sheer size kept them together. Ecosystems in themselves, they played host to many species of plants and animals: *Polypodium* ferns, *Sesuvium* bushes and *Scalesia* trees from the plant kingdom; reptiles, amphibians and even small mammals from the animal world. Eventually, the rivers led to the sea, and as these miniature islands floated farther into open water, they were caught in the prevailing currents and moved quickly away from the mainland.

The probability that any of these rafts would strike the relatively small lava shores of the Galápagos Islands in the world's largest ocean is infinitesimal. And the odds against any animals surviving their protracted time at sea are almost as great. Yet the abundance of life on the Galápagos indicates that some did complete the journey and then survived the rigorous climate, adapting to the merciless heat through evolution.

While the only mammals native to the islands are two kinds of bats and a number of rice rat species, the reptile class is well represented in the Galápagos. Indeed, the islands derived their name from one of their most prominent members, the tortoise, or *galápago*. Reptiles are well suited to withstand the hardships of a long excursion across open ocean: their skin is relatively impermeable; they drink very little fresh water; and their eggs are more resistant to desiccation than those of amphibians (which are absent from the Galápagos Islands). As biologist Ian Thornton points out in his book *Darwin's Islands*, only five successful landings in a time span of one million years (one every 250,000 years) would be sufficient to account for the existence of the

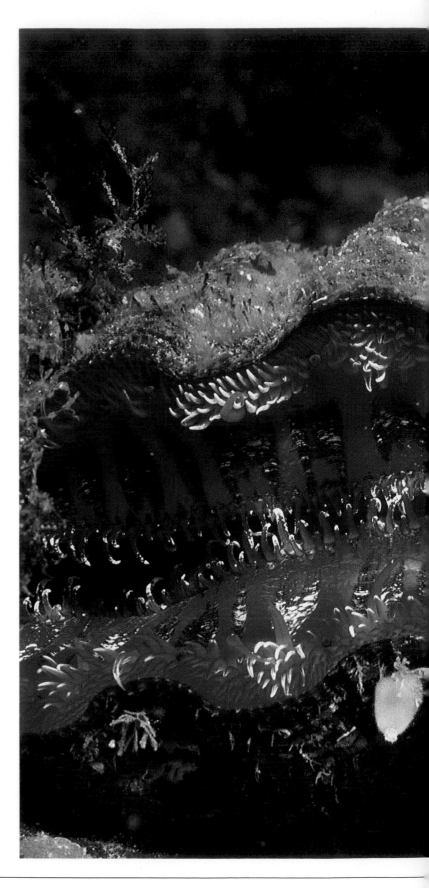

A rock scallop (*Lyropecten* sp) opens its shell to reveal its bright red mantle. Unlike most bivalves, the scallop can travel quite effectively, propelling itself by expelling water from its shell in jetlike squirts.

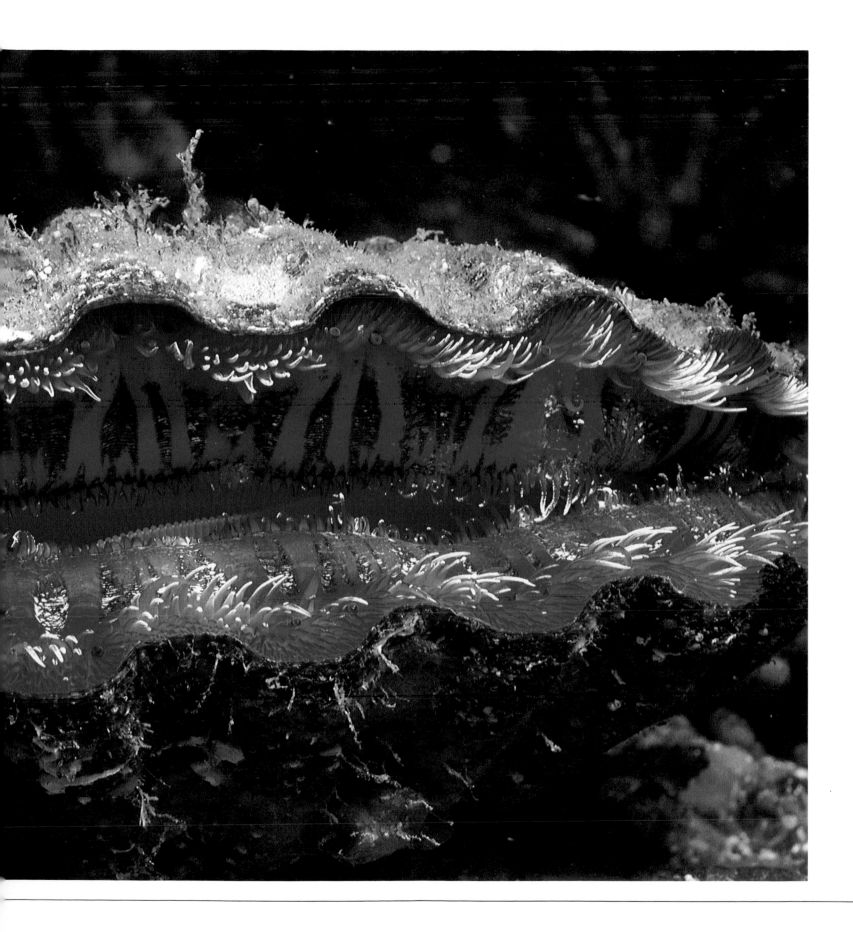

As part of the courtship ritual, a male frigate bird (*Fregata minor*) inflates its throat patch. The frigate is one of 19 marine birds that populate the islands, nesting on the volcanic plateaus and feeding from the sea.

present Galápagos reptiles. The ancestors of the bizarre marine iguanas that I was on my way to photograph no doubt travelled the same stretch of ocean I was crossing to reach the Galápagos Islands, perhaps on rafts or maybe simply drifting helplessly in the currents that sweep west from the continent.

I awoke early the morning of our third day out of Guayaquil and went topside to witness the sun's ascent above the eastern horizon. Some boobies and frigate birds had come to investigate the ship, their presence indicating that we were not far from land. Around noon, I saw in the distance what appeared to be a gelatinous blob floating upon the sea: the Galápagos mist was reducing the easternmost island of San Cristóbal to a ghostly vision. As we drew nearer and shapes became more concrete, I was treated to my first view of the Galápagos Islands.

Over the next three days aboard the *Bucanero*, I caught a glimpse of the terrestrial animals and plants of the Galápagos. As impressive a spectacle as this was, the highlight for me was a visit to a small ring of jagged rocks known as Devil's Crown,

scarcely a quarter-mile off the north shore of Isla Floreana. Nowhere in the Galápagos would I witness a more poignant contrast between the topside and underwater scenery, a sort of heaven and hell in reverse. The jet-black lava was almost sinister in its barrenness, while just below the surface of the sea, a thriving kaleidoscopic wonderland awaited me. Perhaps William Beebe was referring to this spot during his 1923 oceanographic expedition when he wrote, "Life beneath the surface . . . presents as great a contrast to the creatures of the land as the fauna of a tropical jungle differs from that of the Arctic."

I got my first taste of the islands' submarine treasures at Devil's Crown during one of the *Bucanero*'s occasional snorkeling trips. The seafloor was sculpted, encrusted with ochre-hued algae. Each crevice was a haven for some form of benthic life — a sea urchin here, a venomous *Conus* with its smooth dappled shell there and a bright, almost fluorescent-orange sea star close by. I watched dozens of timid squirrelfish form a curtain of reds and yellows at the mouth of a black cavern, while a Galápagos sea lion rock-

Appearing from below as a headless denizen of the deep, a marine iguana (*Amblyrhynchus cristatus*) glides through the water. Iguanas seldom have to swim more than 100 feet from shore to feed on algae.

eted through a school of chromis, scattering silver specks in the greenish blue sea. More so than in any other underwater retreat, I felt a real sense of belonging, as though I were not an intruder but, rather, a new and interesting marine species. Instead of fear, the animals showed a strong curiosity. As I reluctantly swam back to the boat, a tight formation of 9 or 10 spotted rays gracefully winged their way by me.

We spent three days cruising the islands of Santiago, Isabela and Fernandina before dropping anchor at my final destination, Academy Bay, Isla Santa Cruz, site of the Charles Darwin Research Station. Academy Bay forms a sweeping semicircle, each end defined by a rocky point, with the squat cement buildings of Puerto Ayora crowding its rugged shore. To the east are the low whitewashed offices and living quarters of the research station, and at the opposite end of the bay is the community known as the European Village. In between are the stores, hotels and houses of the 2,500 local residents. Behind it all, rolling green hills lead to the highlands.

I ferried my crates to the wharf at the Charles Darwin Research Station only to discover that the station's director, Dr. Köster, had resigned three months before my arrival and that his replacement, Günter Reck, had little time for me. I showed him a copy of my hard-won permission from the Galápagos National Park Service to travel through the islands. Despite there being no expiry date on it, he dismissed it as outdated and told me I would need new permission. He walked away abruptly, leaving me in the hands of the assistant director.

I had to return to Quito, the capital, to have my permission updated by the director of parks for Ecuador. This delayed my diving for several weeks, as I had to meet my family in Quito and I did not want to fly to the mainland twice.

I fared well with the mainland bureaucrats, and my first dive in May 1984 at Rocas Gordon, after four years of waiting, made the tribulations of getting under way fade from my mind.

Clinging to an underwater rock face now kept all thought of permits, bureaucrats and bribes from my mind, and as I pushed off from my perch to drop to 60 feet, I turned to the business at hand. The rock face was a gigantic sculpture of convoluted crevices that offered a base for invertebrates and a refuge for fish. Clusters of barnacles, fused to the lava, swept the water with their delicate net of cirri to trap tiny plankton drifting through the sea. Yet except for the barnacles and a few sponges and hydroids, there was little sea life, probably due to negligible current action, which

The beauty of white-tipped hydroids atop an orange sponge disguises their deadly nature. The hydroids' dainty appendages are lined with stinging cells that stun their plankton prey on contact.

Although it resembles a plant, this featherlike branch is actually a colony of several hundred stinging hydroids that feed on plankton carried within reach by the current.

Tom McHugh/Steinhart Aquarium

meant that food was seldom carried past the area. In the hope of finding more subjects to photograph, I finned toward the exposed eastern coast of the islet.

As I neared the northeast corner, a strong current forced me back. I spotted a broad cleft in a wall only 20 feet ahead, and with my camera and strobe tucked under my left arm, I was able to pull myself along the lava cliff to the calmer water at its mouth. Happy to be out of reach of the tidal flow, I swam in farther to explore the gash.

The sunlight began to fade as I penetrated deeper into the crevice, so I switched on the spotting light atop my strobe. In its beam, the menacing face of a green moray eel, with its fierce bullet eyes and a formidable row of sharp teeth, peered out from beneath an overhang.

I continued my passage into the rift until a five-foot Galápagos shark, momentarily cornered by my approach, shot past me to open water, its belly coming within inches of my head. I scanned the water nervously for the presence of others, and in the distance, I could make out shadows of more sharks patrolling the water. What at first I thought were two or three grew rapidly to five or six, then seven or eight. I drifted in retreat toward the entrance, keeping my back against the rocks.

The sharks did not seem threatening and at first maintained a distance of 15 to 20 feet, but I was concerned because I could not keep them all in sight. As I watched two sharks swim closer to my flippers, a third skimmed above me, eyes and head appearing out of nowhere. It was time to leave. Still, I hesitated to make a move that would separate me from the safety of the wall behind. Tales of shark attacks on divers rushing to the surface flashed through my mind. I pushed off from the rocks and began swimming toward the outline of the Zodiac, 50 feet above. With long, easy kicks, I reached the inflatable and scrambled aboard.

I had never before caught more than a glimpse of a large shark underwater, and in retrospect, I realize that I acted with unwarranted apprehension. During the rest of my stay in the Galápagos Islands, I would encounter sharks on virtually every dive, and the main problem was usually how to lure them closer for better photographs.

Had I been diving with a partner at Rocas Gordon, my reaction to the sharks would not have been so negative. If nothing else, the presence of a companion offers a sense of security. In my haste to proceed with an already delay-ridden assignment, I had ignored my own policy about never diving alone in unfamiliar waters. My first dive at Rocas Gordon convinced me that the combination of bottom topography, marine life and unpredictable currents precluded diving solo in the Galápagos Islands.

Although a partner would increase my daily expenses, already a strain on my budget, I knew that I could not continue without assistance and that I had travelled too far to give up so easily. We turned back to Puerto Ayora to find a diving partner.

The occasional unheralded appearance of one of the area's 24 shark species was unnerving. Although natural food supplies were plentiful, I sometimes wished I had taken a "shark billy" along for protection.

A longnose hawkfish (*Oxycirrhites typus*) darts past a colourful assortment of bottom-dwelling invertebrates and a stand of black coral (*Antipathes galapagensis*) encrusted with yellow polyps.

Aboard the Normita

Slow crawls and quick descents
in the central islands

Puerto Ayora, the largest of nine villages in the Galápagos Islands and populated by enterprising Ecuadorians and several dozen eccentric foreigners, is the islands' commercial centre, the natural consequence of a thriving tourist industry that has blossomed in the past 20 years. Longtime resident Karl Angermeyer can remember when only a few hundred people made their home on Isla Santa Cruz and visitors were a rarity. Karl and his two brothers, Fritz and Gus, were among the original inhabitants of this island, having fled Germany just prior to World War II. At first, they lived in the humid highlands, where they were able to grow crops such as sugarcane, bananas, papayas, coffee and citrus fruits in abundance. However, as supply boats pulled into Academy Bay with greater frequency, the islanders became less dependent on their own resources. This allowed the Angermeyers to move down to the south coast, where they built new houses at the western fringe of town. Separated from the rest of the village by an inlet, this community is the Upper Manhattan of Puerto Ayora, an exclusive enclave of Europeans,

most of whom have lived in the Galápagos Islands for decades.

The Charles Darwin Research Station is a tiny colony in itself, sprawled over several acres at the eastern extremity of Puerto Ayora. It includes laboratories and storage huts, offices and a library, residences for visiting scientists and photographers, housing for the administrative staff, and tourist attractions such as the small natural-history museum, Von Straelen Hall, and a display, in a circular hut, of young tortoises that represents species peculiar to specific islands in the Galápagos archipelago. The station even has its own power generator and huge cisterns to collect and store precious rainwater, the only source of potable water on Isla Santa Cruz.

Between the station and the European settlement are the hovels of the resident Ecuadorians. The businesses and services to sustain the 2,500 residents of Puerto Ayora stretch out along the network of dirt and crushed-lava roadways. In addition to the town offices and naval headquarters, there are a variety of churches, a bank, a medical clinic-cum-hospital, travel agencies and numerous cafés

36

A barge, laden with supplies brought in by cargo ship from mainland Ecuador, makes its way into Academy Bay. The Galápagos' isolation is an inescapable fact of island life and can turn what, by mainland

standards, would be a simple request for engine parts or camera equipment into a logistical nightmare; new residents soon learn to improvise.

Academy Bay, filled with pleasure and fishing boats, is the site of Puerto Ayora, largest of nine Galápagos villages and launch point for most excursions into the islands.

and hotels. One can send and receive mail, hire a taxi and go to the movies; however, there are no telephones and no television. The village has diesel-generated power from 6 a.m. until midnight, and the domestic supply of brackish water is pumped through the primitive plastic piping system between 7 a.m. and noon.

By mainland standards, the townspeople are well off. Children enjoy access to primary and secondary schools, and there seem to be jobs and a steady flow of foreign currency and visitors from which most people can derive an income. Yet behind the façade of relative prosperity, most people are poor. They struggle daily against entrepreneurs who operate stores and supply houses on a functional but ruthless supply-and-demand basis. Staples such as cooking gas, diesel, gasoline and even drinking water are invariably in short supply and fetch prices far beyond the reach of many families.

Puerto Ayora has as its economic base a mixture of cottage industries and international tourism. Foreigners who now reside in Ecuador, plus a few nationals, have cornered the tourist market, and those who are prospering do so through hard work. The logistics of running an efficient tourist operation in the Galápagos are not simple, so visitors must pay hefty prices for a glimpse of the unusual flora and fauna of the islands. While it is not entirely disagreeable to have tourists pay a premium to experience the Galápagos Islands, it is being carried to such an extreme that many vacationers are spending money on more affordable destinations, and the swelling number of tourists during the 1970s has begun a gradual decline. As those involved in the tourist industry start to cater to fewer and more discriminating customers, it becomes clear that without the tourist trade, Puerto Ayora would be nothing more than an outpost that could support only a small population.

My immediate problem was to find an affordable diving companion, and like every other visitor to the Galápagos, I found myself at the mercy of the Puerto Ayora economy. The local diving guides charged $35 to $50 (U.S.) a day, making a good living from the expensive cruise boats that frequented the area,

but for my prolonged excursion, it was too much to pay. Aboard the *Normita*, the image of a dozen sharks still fresh in my mind, we talked about the alternatives, and Juan and Jorgé agreed to contact some diver friends. Shortly after dropping anchor in Academy Bay, they went ashore to track them down, and Juan returned not half an hour later with Mario Possa, a certified park guide in his early twenties.

Quiet and reserved, Mario blends in with the ambience of the Galápagos. Apart from a few years of senior high school in Guayaquil, Mario has spent his youth in the islands. Through experience and his training as a park guide, his knowledge of above-water Galápagos is extensive. But more important to me, he had worked with an American team of oceanographers in the island waters and was therefore familiar with the subtidal Galápagos.

Mario was keen to work and hurried off to collect his travelling kit and a wet suit. Within a few hours of our return, we were weighing anchor to motor away from Puerto Ayora once more.

En route to our planned night mooring at Islas Plazas, 12 miles away, I pondered the amazing collection of islands that make up the Galápagos archipelago and the fascination it holds for man.

The Galápagos Islands, with a total landmass of 3,090 square miles, appear on most maps as small specks on the equator beside the giant relief of South America. There are literally thousands of islands and island groups sprinkled across the wide Pacific, but the Galápagos ecosystem has attracted more attention than the others due to the presence of unusual plants and animals, a presence mainly attributable to the massive ocean currents that bathe the archipelago.

A general understanding of currents and oceanography is necessary to grasp the role the ocean plays in the Galápagos. Because Earth spins on its axis in an easterly direction, water at the equator flows from east to west, the Pacific waters eventually running into, and being deflected by, the Asian continent. Waters to the south of the equator are forced southward and then eastward along the lower reaches of the Pacific Ocean, whereas waters to the north

Curious sea lions (*Zalophus californianus wollebaeki*) jostle for position as I explore near their rookery at Islas Plazas. With winglike front flippers and hind-limb rudders, they are probably the sea's most agile swimmers.

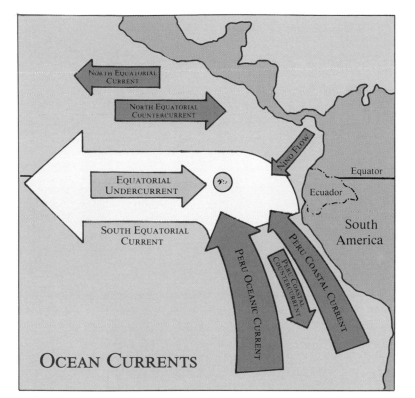

OCEAN CURRENTS

Map labels: NORTH EQUATORIAL CURRENT; NORTH EQUATORIAL COUNTERCURRENT; NIÑO FLOW; EQUATORIAL UNDERCURRENT; SOUTH EQUATORIAL CURRENT; PERU OCEANIC CURRENT; PERU COASTAL COUNTERCURRENT; PERU COASTAL CURRENT; Equator; Ecuador; South America

of the equator move clockwise. The circuit is completed as the southern waters flow north along the west coast of South America and then west along the equator once again. The northern waters are turned southward as they run against the North American continent, continue past Central America and then course westward.

The Galápagos Islands are situated at the intersection of these major currents, and while many currents have played a role in shaping the natural history of these islands, the major influences are the Peru Current, the South Equatorial Current and the Equatorial Undercurrent, also known as the Cromwell Current. These three systems alone move 18.7 billion imperial gallons of water per second, a rate of flow that would completely drain the Great Lakes in just under an hour.

The Peru Current is a complex system of coastal currents, countercurrents and undercurrents. Of these, the Peru Oceanic Current and the Peru Coastal Current exercise an influence on the Galápagos. The Peru Oceanic Current carries relatively cool

Descendant of Antarctic penguins carried to the islands centuries ago by the Humboldt Current, this Galápagos penguin (*Spheniscus mendiculus*) ventures along the volcanic shore in search of shade.

(68 to 75 degrees F), subtropical and highly saline offshore waters from Peru and Chile in a northwesterly direction until it reaches the equator and turns westward to become part of the South Equatorial Current.

The Peru Coastal Current is also known as the Humboldt Current, named for German explorer and geographer Alexander von Humboldt, who described it during his expedition to Central and South America from 1799 to 1804. This is biotically fertile water that extends up to 400 miles off South America's west coast, and although it represents only about 0.2 percent of the world's ocean area, it has been responsible for as much as 22 percent of the annual global fish catch.

As well as all of this circular trans-Pacific flowing, the water also moves vertically in a motion known as upwelling, which accounts for the abundant marine life off the coasts of Chile and Peru. As the surface water moves westward, assisted by the trade winds, cool submarine waters are drawn up to replace it. From the darkness of the bathypelagic regions deep below the surface, nutrients such as phosphates and nitrates are transported to the euphotic zone, where there is sufficient light for photosynthesis. The rich combination of food and light results in a proliferation of phytoplankton, tiny marine algae that provide a food source for the fish stock. In this area, it is mainly anchovies.

The waters of the Peru Coastal Current are quite cool — as low as 59 degrees — for not only does the current begin its northward drive from the Antarctic region, but it is then supplemented by cold source water drawn from the deep reaches of the ocean. The water mass experiences some horizontal and vertical mixing with warmer waters on its way to the Galápagos, but sea temperatures remain between a cool 64 and 72 degrees. Thus, despite straddling the equator, the islands are considered subtropical.

In addition to influencing the climate, the Humboldt Current has also been instrumental in transporting several species of marine fauna to the Galápagos archipelago. Of the islands' known marine forms, approximately 7 percent seem to have originated in Peru or Chile. Certainly, the Humboldt's most distinctive accomplishment has been its part in providing a vehicle for the introduction of penguins to the cactus-studded isles. The Galápagos penguin (*Spheniscus mendiculus*) is closely related to the Magellan penguin of southern Chile, the Falklands and islands near Antarctica, over 4,000 miles away. No other species of penguin can be found living this far north or under conditions so contrary to its customary Antarctic environment.

The driving force behind the Peru Current is the southeast trade winds, which blow strongest from June to December, pushing the ocean waters as they go. The chilly waters carried by this current decrease ambient air temperatures and produce a phenomenon the locals call the *garúa*. As the cool air close to the ocean's surface slips under the normally warm air of this equatorial region, the warmer air cools and releases its moisture as a fine driz-

Habitual nocturnal feeders, tube corals (*Tubastraea* sp) usually stay puckered and closed during daylight hours. Oddly, a solitary blossom remains open, its tentacles stretched out to catch food particles drifting past.

Nighttime dives allowed us the chance to see this tennis-ball-sized group of orange tube corals (*Tubastraea* sp) reach its symmetrical tentacles out to feed on passing plankton. The arms are lined with tiny arrows encased in specialized stinging cells, called nematocysts, which paralyze their prey.

zle. Fogs roll in, and misty conditions are common. Surprisingly, this part of the year is known as the dry season because very little measurable rainfall occurs.

When the trade winds slacken in December and January, the flow of the Peru Current weakens, allowing the warm (75 to 80 degrees) South Equatorial Current to move southward from the Panama Bight. It pulls a warm air mass with it so that the archipelago bakes under clear blue skies and a searing sun during the first six months of each year.

The presence of the majority of marine-animal species is attributable to the tropical South Equatorial Current. Fifty-four percent of the marine life are eastern Pacific species. While some animals originated in the northern Pacific, the coast of California, the Gulf of California and the Caribbean (through the Panama Canal), most are from the Central American Basin near Colombia, Panama and Costa Rica, where the greatest affinities lie between the Galápagos fauna and its ancestral population.

The final major oceanic influence is the Cromwell Current, or Equatorial Undercurrent, a massive subsurface current that moves counter to the prevailing flow of water. Generally found at a depth of 300 feet running from west to east against the South Equatorial Current, it deflects upward as it approaches the landmass of the western Galápagos, bringing its cold and nutrient-rich waters toward the surface. As with upwelling off the Chilean and Peruvian coasts, phytoplankton flourish and marine life abounds. According to Dr. Gerard Wellington of the Marine Science Program at the University of Houston, "This is, perhaps, the most unique current affecting the archipelago." During my travels, I would have the opportunity to witness the dramatic effect of the Cromwell Current, as visibility in massive areas of the ocean would be obscured by phytoplankton.

The Galápagos Islands (including the far northern islands of Darwin and Wolf) are spread over a 35,000-square-mile chunk of the eastern Pacific Ocean, and with so many current systems, it is not surprising that some islands have richer sea life than others. Habitat variability and differences in water temperature, salinity and productivity from one region of the archipelago to another restrict the distribution of some marine species. For example, the Moorish idol (*Zanclus cornutus*) and sunset wrasse (*Thalassoma lutescens*) are common in the northern region of the Galápagos but are rare or absent in the colder waters of the western sector. Biologists describe this diversification of marine habitats within a defined region of the sea as marine provincialism.

A group of sponges shares a patch of seafloor with a colony of zoanthids. While zoanthids take food from the passing current, sponges draw water into their bodies through skin perforations and extract oxygen and nutrients.

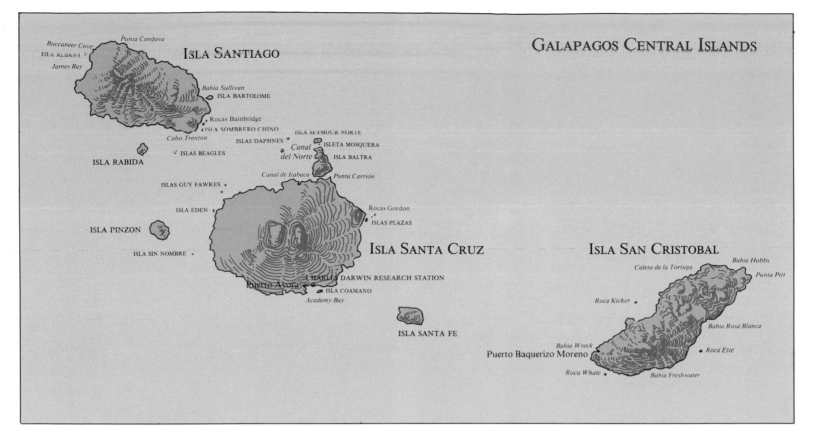

In the Galápagos Islands, it is generally recognized that four marine provinces exist: northern, western, southern and central.

The central marine province is the least distinct of the four sectors in terms of the singularity of the fish and invertebrates. Influenced by most current systems entering the islands, it has a broad representation of marine creatures. The Galápagos penguin, for example, can be found on the south coast of Isla Santiago, although it prefers the cooler waters of the western sector.

It was my goal to explore the central marine province, the region closest at hand, on my first expedition. I planned to circumnavigate Isla Santa Cruz in a counterclockwise direction over a period of a week, making a point of diving at such islands as Plaza Norte, Plaza Sur, Seymour Norte, Baltra, the Daphnes and the Beagles.

The crescent-shaped Islas Plazas were the closest to Puerto Ayora, a 2½-hour journey in the *Normita*, so we decided to head to them first because of our late-afternoon departure. While Plaza Norte is off-limits to visitors, the southern island is one of the standard tourist attractions and the site of a large sea lion rookery. It also offers tourists the rare opportunity to view land iguanas.

That night, we moored in the channel separating the two Plazas. Early the next morning, through the porthole beside my bunk, I watched the sun rise. The quiet of dawn was disturbed periodically by the rumble of bubbles bouncing off the *Normita*'s hull: sea lions were playing games, diving underneath the boat and exhaling, enjoying the rustling sound of air knocking against the hull. I dressed quickly, packed some cameras and rowed the Zodiac to the concrete dock built on Isla Plaza Sur by the national park service for the tour-boat traffic. Sleeping sea lions dotted the shoreline, looking out of place sprawled beneath eight-foottall *Opuntia* cacti. I followed the path that led inland, passing a three-foot-long yellowish brown land iguana languidly munching cactus fruit, spines and all. Often, these dragonlike beasts will roll or scrape the fruit along the ground to remove the spines, but this individual did not make the effort. The land about me was covered in patches of *Sesuvium* bushes, strikingly red against the dark lava. It took only 20 minutes to reach the southern edge where the land drops abruptly to the sea, dozens of yards below. Gulls and blue-footed boobies flew below me, white images against the black ocean. The starkness of the land provided an overwhelming contrast to its rich wildlife, and I lingered atop the cliffs for an hour before starting back.

Later that morning, Mario and I dived at Rocas Gordon, along the same wall I had visited by myself the previous day. I wanted a repeat dive there as much to check out Mario's diving ability as to take photographs. Wall-diving, where the seafloor lies unseen hundreds of feet below, is difficult. Since there is no bottom on which to kneel, a diver must be sufficiently comfortable with himself and his equipment to maintain neutral buoyancy.

Mario and I entered the water along the northern face of the largest rock. Even before the bubbles had cleared, it was obvious that Mario was an accomplished diver. He was at ease in the water, neither fighting to stay in place nor producing a ceaseless stream of exhaled gas—marks of an apprehensive, inexperienced diver. We dived twice at Rocas Gordon that morning, and in contrast to my first adventure there, I was relaxed and able to concentrate on photography. Returning to Puerto Ayora to find a diving companion had been a worthwhile investment of time.

From Rocas Gordon, we aimed for the island of Seymour Norte, north of Santa Cruz. We had hoped to reach it by the middle of the afternoon, but by 3 p.m., we were well short of our goal. The *Normita* was ponderously slow, and the moderate seas, running against us broadside, forced the boat to move at a crawl. In order to squeeze in a dive before dark, we chose to explore a site off the island of Baltra, south of Seymour Norte. The islands of Baltra and Seymour Norte are typical of the older islands in the Galápagos, where a series of fault blocks composed of basaltic lava flows and limestone were laid down beneath the sea and later uplifted. The low flat-top islands are characterized by cliffs rising 30 to 50 feet above the ocean and by a broad base beneath the water that slopes gently out to seas as deep as 3,000 feet.

The captain anchored the *Normita* in the Canal del Norte, which separates Baltra from Seymour Norte. Juan steered the Zodiac toward Baltra, taking us close to a jumble of rocks that appeared to have fallen from the cliff above. Mario and I splashed into the water and followed the bottom in a rather abrupt drop to 50 or 60 feet, where a ledge breaks the decline and eases into deeper water. Overhangs and hollows were ripe with clusters of orange tube corals (anemone-like soft corals) and delicate gorgonians, those multibranched fan-shaped corals named after the three sisters of Greek mythology who had writhing snakes for hair. Two-inch-long brown-and-green-mottled blennies brazenly rushed out of hidden dens only to disappear at my slightest movement. Mario flushed a pufferfish (*Arothron meleagris*) from a cave; the cryptic design of the black-spotted phase differed startlingly from the more common yellow phase of this foot-long fish.

Mario also discovered a few unspent brass shells, a token of the hardware the Americans dumped into the sea when they abandoned their base on the island of Baltra after World War II. They had been denied an extension of their lease on the island because Ecuador was anxious to establish its own base there. Rather than transporting their vehicles and machinery back to the United

Made brazen by its cryptic stripes and the protection of a nearby sea urchin's (*Eucidaris thouarsii*) spines, a blenny (*Ophioblennius steindachneri*) three inches long confronts me on the rocky face of Rocas Gordon.

Summerhans/Photo Researchers, Inc.

States, the army simply airlifted many pieces of equipment over the sea and dropped them into it. While this gave the marine life artificial reefs on which to build new communities, the terrestrial life of Baltra suffered dearly at the hands of the armed forces. The most notable casualty was the land iguana, which was exterminated by troops who used it for target practice. Today, the island houses a small complement of men and women on an Ecuadorian base used for training, communications and the supervision of activity at the airport, which provides a direct link between the Galápagos and Guayaquil.

As Mario and I began our ascent to the surface, I saw a sea turtle approaching. It either did not see me or was very inquisitive, because it swam closer. I watched it through my viewfinder and was about to release the shutter when it veered quickly away, chased by a spirited Galápagos sea lion. These pinnipeds were omnipresent and seemed to take great pleasure in foiling my shots.

That night, we anchored in the Canal de Itabaca, the strait that separates the islands of Baltra and Santa Cruz. The next day, we got under way shortly after 7 a.m. and steamed west through the channel and then on to Isla Seymour Norte. The sun burned off the early-morning cloud cover, and the warmth of its rays was welcomed on this chilly morning. It was the time of the year when the cool waters of the Peru Current begin coming to the fore, and as the wind blew across the water, it picked up the rawness, giving a distinct bite to the morning breeze, despite our being on the equator. I still had trouble adjusting to the drop in temperature.

We rounded the northern shore of Isla Seymour Norte and searched for a spot to dive. Although Mario had dived throughout the archipelago, there were countless locations unfamiliar to him. This is what fascinated me about exploring underwater in the Galápagos Islands: with so much coastline, it would be impossible for any person, in a lifetime of diving, to catch more than a glimpse of the unlimited sites. We bypassed many of the areas where Mario had previously dived, opting for sites where the marine life had likely never before seen man.

The northern coast of Isla Seymour Norte is a jagged mass of basalt that drops from a plateau 15 to 20 feet above the sea. I spotted a tiny bay with a rock bridge at the end that I thought might form the roof of a cave. Mario and I suited up, and with Juan at the controls of the Zodiac, we went to inspect the natural bridge. Hauled up on ledges, five Galápagos fur seals were enjoying the habitat best suited to their needs. Like the Galápagos penguin, these sea mammals have migrated to the islands from

Like thousands of stars in a miniature galaxy, the intricate polyps of a gorgonian coral are extended for feeding. When disturbed by a predator or a passing fish, they retract in an instant.

To facilitate their search for food,
fan-shaped gorgonian corals orient
themselves broadside to prevailing
currents, maximizing their
exposure to plankton, their
microscopic food source.

Underwater caverns are common
due to the islands' volcanic origins,
but the one on Isla Seymour
Norte, with its open ceiling and
slanting shafts of light, was the
most dramatic we encountered
during our dives.

distant cold waters along the path of the Humboldt Current, and they hide from the blazing equatorial sun in the shadowy reaches of rocky coasts. Unlike the Galápagos sea lions, the fur seals are wary of man and do not tolerate his presence. As we approached, they slid simultaneously into the sea.

Mario and I jumped into the water and swam toward the mouth of what I hoped was an underwater cave. The visibility was close to 90 feet, and as we swam beneath the archway, I realized that we had stumbled upon a rare diving location. We penetrated farther into the cave and, after a short swim, entered a circular arena 50 feet in diameter that had at its apex, 10 feet above the ocean's surface, an opening to the sky. A shaft of pure white light plummeted into the sea, cutting a brilliant swath through the water. About 60 feet beyond the natural skylight, the wall began to slope inward, and the cave ended.

There was little variety in the marine life inside the cave. There were a few invertebrates typically found in underwater caverns, such as encrusting sponges, small lacy hydrocorals and orange zoanthids. Spiny lobsters, which seek out crevices, were plentiful, tucked beneath overhangs and backed into small fissures, their long sweeping antennae betraying their presence. The only vertebrates I saw were two juvenile sea lions that dive-bombed us on several occasions and a small school of squirrelfish that occupy caves and rocky crevices during the day, choosing to venture out at night in search of their chief food, crustaceans.

Mario and I returned to the Zodiac, then joined the *Normita* and motored around to the southern side of Isla Seymour Norte to lunch in the calmer waters near the long sandbar called Isleta Mosquera. Sea lions by the dozens were rolled up on Mosquera, their black bodies like ashes against the brilliant white of the sand. The lee side of this protected sandbar is a perfect retreat for a sea lion intent on a place to rest and socialize after a tiring food-seeking expedition to the sea. An established sea lion colony is present there year-round. Unlike the sea lion congregations I had seen and photographed off the coast of British Columbia, the sea lions of the Galápagos were never segregated into male-only groups. Instead, many of the islands were host to small sea lion rookeries, complete with playful pups, protective cows and ruling bulls.

After lunch, I made a brief excursion ashore at Isla Seymour Norte to photograph blue-footed boobies and the aptly named magnificent frigate birds. The tourist trail wends its way through Palo Santo trees, passing within feet of the crude nests that

Nature has ensured that the fancy footwork of the male blue-footed booby (*Sula nebouxii*), left, will catch the eye of the female. In a ponderously slow dance, he lifts each foot in turn until his intended has either joined him or departed.

boobies scrape in the ground. I sat on a rock for at least 20 minutes and watched the elaborate courtship dance of a blue-footed booby. A male was busily trying to impress a female by sky-pointing, simultaneously raising both rear end and beak skyward, partially spreading his wings and emitting a long, reedy whistle. Having captured the female's attention, the male proceeded to show off his webbed delights, alternately lifting each azure foot in a melodramatic display.

I left the boobies to complete their ritual in peace and continued along the path to where some magnificent frigate birds were nesting in the bushes. The magnificent frigate bird is one of two species in the Galápagos, the other being the great frigate bird. The males of both species have large red throat patches that they inflate during the mating season to attract females. Many of the big nests, woven by the female with twigs collected by her mate, cradled the result of a successful mating: a single gawky juvenile.

The heat of midday drove me back to the coast, where I boarded the *Normita* and gave the go-ahead to motor to Caleta Tortuga Negra, a vast mangrove lagoon on the northern coast of Isla Santa Cruz. We anchored the *Normita* off the broad mouth of the lagoon, and Mario and I took the Zodiac into the heart of the mangrove forest.

Caleta Tortuga Negra is a mangrove haven at its best. Dense thickets of red and black mangroves have grown over acres of this lagoon by constantly sending new shoots into the water. The roots trap nutrient-rich sediment and debris from the ocean to form one of the world's most fertile environments.

Birds are especially evident at Caleta Tortuga Negra. Great blue herons nest in the tops of the mangroves where they can drop to the water's edge to feed on any of dozens of species of tiny fish that swim among the tangled roots. Lava herons can often be seen creeping stealthily over the rocks and roots, periodically driving their bills into the water and returning with a wiggling fish. On the surface of the lagoon, brown pelicans paddle about, thrusting bill and pouch underwater, while brown noddies stand on the pelicans' back and neck, picking scraps from whatever gushes out of their hosts' pouch.

Sea turtles, for which this lagoon is named, often rest at the surface, their carapaces appearing as misplaced rocks. The under-water world teems with fish, ranging from large blacktip sharks to schools of baitfish that leap out of the water en masse to escape predation. Golden and spotted eagle rays wing their way through the shallows.

I had wanted to photograph sea turtles and perhaps rays under-water but was frustrated to find the water extremely murky with suspended sediment. Instead, I stowed my underwater housings at the bow of the Zodiac and concentrated on photographing the creatures topside.

Mario guided me through the mangroves, a giant maze of sinu-ous waterways in which I certainly would have become lost if left on my own. But he had directed tourists through this lagoon on numerous occasions and knew exactly where each channel led. He would choose the left fork one time, the right the next. We often had to lie flat against the Zodiac to avoid being snagged by gnarled and twisted branches. It was a venture into a world where plants that were once terrestrial have invaded the sea, and an entire ecosystem has developed because of it. We returned to the mouth of the lagoon just as the sun was setting, soaking the mangrove trees in a reddish orange glow.

That night was spent beneath an equatorial sky ablaze with glittering stars. After supper, I was busy charging strobes and loading cameras for the next day's shoot when Mario called me up to the main deck. Using a flashlight, he had located newly hatched sea turtles swimming past the starboard side of the *Normita*. Barely two inches long, they looked vulnerable in the ink-black sea, fragile immigrants in an inimical new world. I bent down and scooped one from the water. Its strong foreflippers flailed against my outstretched palm in an anxious attempt to

One evening, while moored at the mouth of Caleta Tortuga Negra, I reached overboard and plucked this newly hatched Pacific green sea turtle (*Chelonia mydas agassizii*) from the sea. Having survived the danger of bird predation as it travelled across the beach from its nest, it now faced the perils of the sea.

regain the sea. It was in every way a miniature replica of a mature sea turtle: bulging eyes, hooked beak and an intricately patterned, though more pliant, carapace. It was this soft carapace that would lead almost certainly to the death of this tiny passerby. Until its shell grew and tempered into the firmness of an adult, it would always be in danger. This turtle's chances of reaching that stage were minuscule. Yet it had succeeded after birth in conquering the deadly strip of sand between its nest and the ocean. Now it had to brave the odds and prove itself at sea. I lowered it gently into the water, almost reluctant to let it go, and watched it disappear into the night.

The huge millpond of the Pacific Ocean greeted my sleepy eyes the following morning. Not a ripple disturbed the surface. Having lived for years beside the often tempestuous North Pacific Ocean off Vancouver Island, I found it difficult to accept just how tranquil the sea around the Galápagos Islands can be, especially in the early-morning hours. We left our mooring and steamed toward Islas Daphnes, located north of Isla Santa Cruz and due west of Baltra. Two islands, Daphne and Daphne Minor, plus a small shoal of rocks in between, form this group. We came upon Daphne first, an island which is conical in shape with sides that slope down toward the sea where steep cliffs drop the remaining 50 to 60 feet to the water's edge.

Mario and I dived the south face of Daphne. Underwater, the cliffs continue their plunge to a depth of about 20 feet before they assume a gentler slope into deeper water. The lava face is pitted with caverns where gobies, butterflyfish, bright red squirrelfish and moray eels abound. I was photographing these fish, concentrating on following the moving targets in my viewfinder, when I felt a presence behind me. I turned slowly to meet the wide-set eyes of a giant manta ray. This huge member of the ray family, named for its resemblance in shape to a loose cloak, or manta, was hovering 15 feet away, leisurely flapping its "wings" to maintain its position. At first glance, the demeanour of this 18-foot monster was entirely menacing—long fleshy appendages projected from either side of its broad mouth. Seafarers of old called it the devilfish and spun tales of the manta's malevolence and of how fellow seamen had been swallowed whole by these evil creatures. Dead seamen are excellent food for many a myth.

It is interesting how in the sea, the largest creatures feed on the smallest animals. Like the biggest cetaceans (blue whales) and the grandest of sharks (the whale shark *Rhincodon*), the greatest of rays, the manta, also dines by filtering small animals from the sea.

To date, the unregulated harvest of lobster beds has put the spiny lobster (*Panulirus gracilis*) at risk in the Galápagos. Thousands are caught annually by local fishermen who ship them to markets on the mainland.

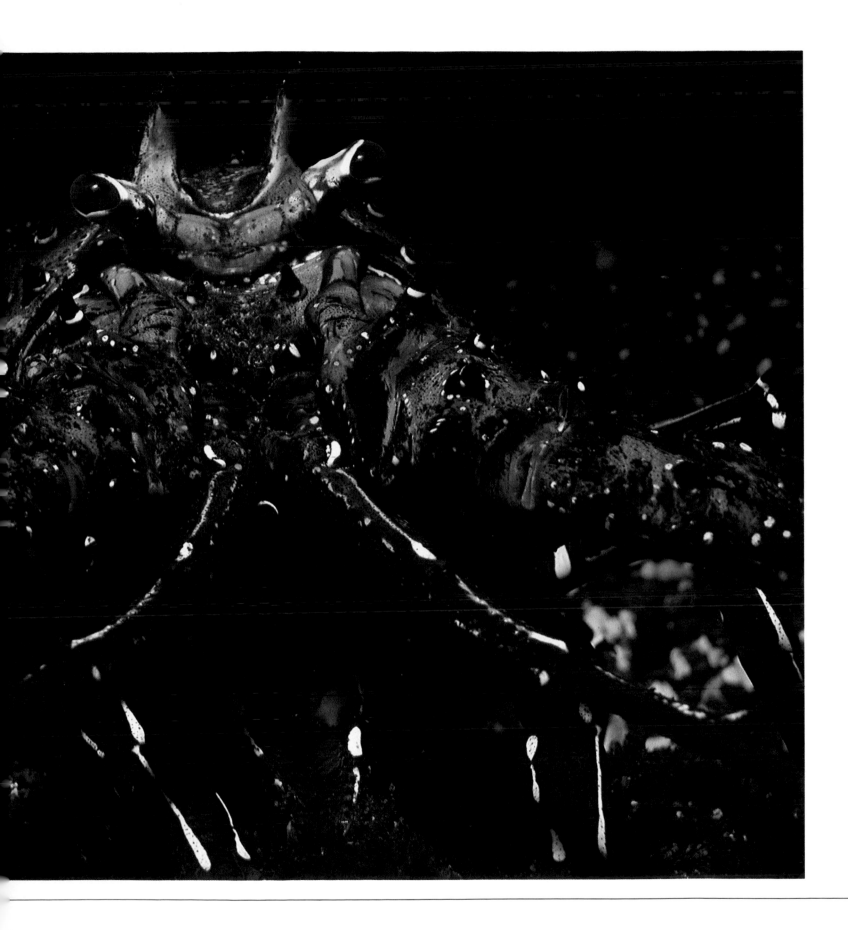

The cephalic fins on either side of the manta's mouth are highly mobile and are believed to be extended by the manta during feeding, acting to funnel water and plankton into its mouth. When water enters the mouth, it encounters a complex filter system where small animals are trapped and subsequently swallowed. Large and bony seamen would simply not be considered food by a manta, but mantas have been known to overturn light boats after being harpooned.

Our encounter seemed longer than it actually was: seconds would be more accurate than minutes. Yet it was one of those uncommon times when a diver is granted the rare sighting of a mysterious animal of the sea. And what made it all the more special was that I knew our curiosity was mutual. The manta ray did not come so near nor stay so long for only my benefit, and as it swam away, I knew it would return.

I motioned for Mario to bring my camera with the wide-angle lens so that I could photograph this behemoth in its entirety when it came back. The visibility was poor — 40 feet horizontally at best — so I needed the wide-angle lens to photograph the manta ray as closely as possible. We exchanged camera housings, and I swam away from shore until I was floating 35 feet below the surface.

What a peculiar feeling, drifting as I was, slowly spinning in the water with my eyes straining past the limits of visibility to see the manta ray. A grey shadow approached but veered away before materializing into solid flesh. Was this the manta or some other large creature that had come to investigate? Then, wraithlike, out of the dark screen of my limited vision, a manta ray appeared, flapping its wings like a man rowing a dinghy, straining alternately on each oar. I rose 20 feet to meet the ray and photographed it as it swam by.

Two remoras had secured themselves close to the ray's mouth, and the sight of these fish gave a hint of the manta's largeness. The remoras were two feet long, yet they looked like minnows beside their unwitting host. The remora belongs to the group of fish known as commensals, meaning "those who eat at the same

A moray eel (*Lycodontis castaneus*), with a reputation as a ferocious biter, swings its head toward me. Moray eels breathe by opening and closing their mouths, which makes them appear more menacing than they are.

A lava heron (*Butorides sundevalli*) takes advantage of its perch in a mangrove lagoon at Caleta Tortuga Negra to search for prey. These lagoons are an important link in the intertidal zone between land and sea, the tree branches providing nesting sites for birds and the roots attracting the crustaceans and schools of small fish on which the birds feed.

Spikes bristling, a five-armed sea
star (*Nidoriella armata*) plods
slowly across the seafloor. The sea
star does not live up to its
formidable appearance, however,
as its spikes are soft and pliable
and it feeds on small crustaceans.

table." It attaches itself to whales, manta rays or sharks by means of a suction disc on the top of its head and lives on the scraps from its hosts' meals. Despite the tagalongs, the manta ray moved with a majestic elegance.

During the next 10 to 15 minutes, I enjoyed repeated visits from this manta ray as well as another. There may actually have been more, but I saw only two at any one time. Eventually, I ran out of film, and they apparently sated their curiosity. Twice more during my stay in the Galápagos Islands, I would swim with manta rays, but the encounters would be fleeting, without the interplay that characterized this first meeting.

Mario and I returned to the *Normita* to fill our scuba tanks and eat lunch. We then dived the east side of Daphne. The gently sloping bottom was strewn with boulders. Several Galápagos sharks made themselves known, and I was able to photograph some pretty trumpetfish and damselfish, but the dive was a disappointment overall, for we saw few other species. Mario and I stayed submerged less than half an hour before returning to the *Normita* for the short run over to Daphne Minor.

I was beginning to see how bottom topography related to the amount and diversity of undersea creatures. Generally, I found that areas of steep drop-offs into water hundreds of feet deep offered a more exciting dive than sites where the bottom sloped gently out to sea and was littered with boulders. Upwelling and swifter currents carry with them greater quantities of food that can support more bottom-dwelling creatures, and these conditions seemed to prevail in areas of sharp declines. With the rare exception of Devil's Crown in the southern marine province, this generalization holds true for most of the islands.

Daphne Minor juts straight out of the sea. It appears to be older than Daphne, for the original volcanic cone has been worn smooth, leaving the island with the appearance of a bald head atop sheer cliffs. It is a favourite nesting ground of the red-billed tropicbird, a striking seabird with a predominantly white body, coral-red beak and two very fine long plumes that trail behind. The shape of its tail allows the tropicbird to shift direction upward or downward rapidly, so it can rise and dive with surprising agility. It can often be seen out at sea plunging into the water from heights of 50 to 70 feet to catch fish. The tropicbird is most active around twilight when, in the relative darkness, its preferred food of squid comes to the surface.

Subtidally, the south side of Daphne Minor continues straight down as far as the eye can see. Lava walls are fashioned in the

sculpted patterns common throughout the Galápagos. Along this face, virtually every benthic organism of the central islands can be found: slipper lobsters, crabs, corals, sponges, ascidians, sea stars and mollusks (including octopuses) are crammed into the rocky crevices. I cursed the physiology of the human body because, with all the dives we had logged that day, we had to limit ourselves to diving no deeper than 40 feet if we wished to spend much time underwater. I wanted to discover what existed another 20 to 50 feet below, but to do so meant chancing the bends.

Decompression sickness, or the bends, occurs when nitrogen gas that has been absorbed into body tissue under the pressure of a dive is released too rapidly as a diver ascends. If a diver goes from the high pressure of the deep to the low pressure of the surface too quickly, the nitrogen gas bubbles and expands in the bloodstream and can impede the flow of oxygen and nutrients to vital tissues. The rate of nitrogen absorption by the tissues is a factor in how long and to what depth one can dive. A dive table published by the U.S. Navy indicates how much time a person

In the waters off Isla Daphne, an 18-foot-wide giant Pacific manta ray (*Manta hamiltoni*) wings by, two-foot-long remoras (*Remora* sp) clinging to its mouth. Sailors call it the devilfish, but it is more curious than dangerous.

can spend at a certain depth and still be able to return directly to the surface. If these limits are exceeded, there is a real chance of becoming afflicted with the painful and sometimes deadly bends. There is only one treatment for decompression sickness: a recompression chamber, which simulates the pressures encountered in diving underwater, consequently forcing nitrogen back into solution in the body. And the recompression chamber closest to the Galápagos Islands is in Panama City, 1,000 miles away. Such a distance would necessitate flying, subjecting the diver to even lower atmospheric pressures. Therefore, I had to monitor precisely the time and depth of each dive to avoid the risk.

The sun was dropping quickly toward the western horizon when Mario and I surfaced. There is no place to moor for the night at the Daphnes, so we motored back to the north shore of Isla Santa Cruz to pass the night. The following morning, the fourth day of our trip, we left for the south coast of Isla Santiago.

It started out as just a day of uneventful cruising, but within the first hour, I was brought to life. "Whales!" I cried as dorsal fins broke the surface like a dozen missiles launched as one. Against the sun's oblique rays, drops of spray sparkled like sequins, and puffs of mist obscured the air directly above the pod. The captain shook his head and shouted, "*Delfin, delfin!*" The old man's eyesight was failing, for these animals were too big and were moving too slowly to be dolphins.

The pod of 60 to 80 pilot whales was swimming directly toward us from not more than 75 to 100 yards away. We stopped the *Normita*, and Mario pulled the Zodiac alongside as I hurried to grab cameras, mask, fins and snorkel. The whales were almost upon us by this time, and I feared that any delay in preparing scuba tank and regulator might jeopardize my chance to swim with these mystical mammals of the sea. I hopped into the Zodiac, and Mario sped us toward the pod, now only 15 yards away. As we came abreast, I could hear the whoosh of exhaled air.

The whales surrounded the boat, surfacing, diving and pacing us. I rolled overboard and floated at the surface, breathing hard from the sobering shock of cold water. I could hear the whales communicating, sounding like the creak of barn-door hinges in need of oil, but I could see nothing except the sun's rays fanning out beneath the waves. I had taken the whales by surprise, and they were wary now that I had entered their domain. We humans are visual creatures, and I longed for a sighting; yet at the same time, I felt marvellously at ease, floating in the midst of the whales' haunting cries.

A hermit crab (*Aniculus elegans*) slowly emerges from its shell, using its flexible eye stalks to check for danger. These crabs seek refuge in abandoned shells, upgrading to larger ones as their bodies grow.

to the southeast. Two hours later, we dropped anchor in the small cove formed by the two largest islands of the group and a meagre spit that bridges the gap between them at the west end. Great horizontal streaks scar the rock faces, giving some indication of the tumult and strain that accompanied the birth of both these islets. Sea lions are abundant there, basking in the sun on the sand spit at low tide. As the tide rises, they are forced to leave the spit and make their way up the steep flanks of the islands in search of drier ground. At night, we saw some sea lions 40 to 50 feet up the hills, far higher than is necessary to escape the tides. Their willingness to sleep so far from the sea indicates how unconcerned they are about predators.

Late that afternoon, Mario and I suited up and entered the water on the northeast side of the southern island. Like Rocas Gordon, the wall is precipitous, the bottom unseen. Once again, because of previous dives that day, we had to limit our depth to 40 feet. Nevertheless, we found a world replete with marine life. Great vertical fissures, some large enough for us to fit inside, were painted with all colours of encrusting sponges and both hard and soft corals. At our maximum depth, we came across a few bushes of hard Panamanian black coral as well as the softer endemic Galápagos black coral. Hard corals generally prefer deeper water, and these few bushes were a promising omen of what might exist 40 to 50 feet below us. I decided that we should dive this same spot the following morning when our bodies would be free of excess nitrogen and we could safely dive deeper.

So at 8 a.m. on the last day of our trip, Mario and I rolled over the side of the Zodiac and plunged down the sheer rock face. At 60 feet, more bushes of black coral were evident; at 80 feet, large patches of corals clung to the rocks; at 100 feet, we were engulfed in a meadow of yellow and reddish brown black corals. I felt like a 10-year-old in the prairies who is barely able to peer above a sea of golden wheat. Schools of grunts sandwiched us between them and the corals; cryptic longnose hawkfish blended in with the coral branches; morays and lobsters filled the cracks; a sea turtle dogged us the whole dive. The scene was straight from a child's fantasies about the sea.

Black corals are just one family in a group of cnidarians known as precious corals. Distributed mainly in tropical waters, precious corals are found at depths from a hundred to a few thousand feet below the surface. Unlike shallow-water coral species, which are porous and too soft for jewellery production, precious corals are often as hard as ivory and almost imperishable. They can be

66

Stalks of hard Panamanian black coral (*Antipathes panamensis*), hidden beneath reddish polyps, provide a source of cash for locals. While the coral is ideal for carving souvenirs, its slow rate of growth carries a high environmental cost.

carved into beautiful necklaces, rings, brooches and pendants and have spawned a worldwide industry estimated to be worth $800 million a year.

Man's fascination with precious corals predates the 20th century. Corals have been found together with human remains from Palaeolithic times; the ancient Greeks believed red coral to be a source of immortality. But now, as advancing technology moves man more easily into the deeper reaches of the sea—the regions where precious corals thrive—these slow-growing animal colonies are being harvested at an alarming rate. The waters surrounding the Galápagos Islands are one of the few areas in the world where black corals still grow in abundance, but they, too, would be lost if the harvest were to continue unchecked. The black coral colonies of Hawaii and the Caribbean are already seriously depleted.

There were inhabitants of the villages of Puerto Ayora, Isla Santa Cruz, and Puerto Baquerizo Moreno, Isla San Cristóbal, who were removing black coral wherever they found it. No thought was being given to selective harvesting; instead, the rockhard coral limbs were falling indiscriminately to fine-toothed saws to become raw material for the craftsmen's files. Black corals grow very slowly—only about 2½ inches per year—so it will take decades to replace the broomstick-thick stalks sought by the artisans, if the corals survive at all.

Local skilled craftsmen coaxed delicate figures of sea lions, whales and penguins from the rough coral branches and buffed them to a glass-smooth finish. As each cruise ship dropped anchor in Academy Bay and disgorged its complement of tourists, shops swung wide their doors, and youngsters weighted down with black coral wares lined the parched streets. Many visitors, while applauding the conservation efforts in the Galápagos Islands, purchased dozens of these souvenirs, heedless of the requests of naturalists not to do so. The hypocrisy was appalling.

The sight of black corals in nature would have quickly convinced most tourists to shun the trinket hawkers of Puerto Ayora, for they are the city structures of the undersea world, major building blocks in the sea upon which many marine creatures depend for their existence. The pieces of black coral, carved into figurines and polished to a high sheen, once grew in the sea and provided a haven for hawkfish, a foundation for pelagic zooplankton and a base for marauding nudibranchs.

It was difficult to reconcile the strict protection of the terrestrial wildlife of the Galápagos Islands with the open harvest and sale of black coral. Yet it is not surprising, for the Galápagos National

A school of creolefish (*Paranthias fercifer*) storms the walls of Islas Beagles in search of zooplankton on the lava rock face. Strangely, one of their greatest competitors is the stationary stands of black coral (*Antipathes panamensis*).

Park Service had no jurisdiction below the tide line and was therefore helpless to stop this oceanic plunder. It is little wonder that the park service wanted to extend its control to the reaches of this archipelago's subtidal zones.

The realities of air supply and decompression schedules imposed themselves on my coral reverie, and we began our slow ascent to the *Normita*, satisfied with our dive and convinced of the need to preserve this paradise.

As we began our journey back to Puerto Ayora, I watched with regret as Islas Beagles grew more distant in our wake. I would have loved to spend a week exploring just this group of islands, but time would not permit it. I also had to put on hold my investigation of Isla Santiago. Prior to leaving on this trip, I had made plans with marine biologist Jack Grove to accompany me on an expedition to the western marine province, and I had to get back to make arrangements for that trip. Mario had previously committed himself to work on another charter as well,

and so we both needed to reach Puerto Ayora by that evening.

To break the monotony of the trip back to port, I decided to dive at Islas Guy Fawkes off the northwest coast of Santa Cruz. The three islands have tall cliffs of striated rock, their bases eroded over the centuries by stormy seas. We motored close to an islet with a large pinnacle, jumped into the water and worked our way slowly down the steep drop-off. We had to limit ourselves to 50 feet because of our deep dive at Islas Beagles that morning, but it was obvious that this was another site particularly rich in black corals. The fish life was abundant, and while I was photographing a large school of jacks, a manta ray winged past.

The dive completed, we headed home down the west coast of Isla Santa Cruz. The variety of marine creatures I had encountered during the week of diving had whetted my appetite for further exploration, and as we neared Puerto Ayora, I was already planning the itinerary for my trip to the western sector of the Galápagos Islands.

A five-foot-long moray eel (*Lycodontis castaneus*) peers around the stalks of a Galápagos black coral bush (*Antipathes galapagensis*). Morays hide in crevices by day and emerge at night to hunt.

Anemones (*Bunobactis mexicana*),
the size of golf balls, thrive in tide
pools on the rocky shoreline. Each
tide brings a change of water and
fresh supplies of plankton.

Island of Fire

Discovering the subtidal secrets
of a western volcanic giant

D ue to the remoteness of the Galápagos Islands, the simplest routine tends to take an inordinate amount of time, and the most basic services seem a luxury. For example, a minor problem with my outboard motor resulted in a six-hour search of Puerto Ayora for a mechanic with the necessary tools to weld a piece of steel to the "shifter-dog" to stop the engine from jumping out of gear. To obtain gasoline for running the outboard and compressor, I had to hire a truck, buy an empty 45-gallon drum, drive to the municipal storage area in town, trade in the empty drum and purchase a full one, load the full tank onto the pickup truck, drive to our house and roll the drum 100 feet down the winding path to the workshop. There, I ingested a tablespoon or two of gasoline before finally coaxing it to siphon through the hose into jerry cans. Upon my return to the mainland, I stared at gas pumps with newfound admiration.

It took more time to arrange for the replacement of two underwater strobes that had failed. Having new strobes shipped from Canada posthaste was not a simple matter of picking up a telephone and dialing the overseas operator. The only telephone service on the island of Santa Cruz is radio phone, which can reach mainland Ecuador only marginally, and callers stand in line to get the operator. Once, I waited two hours in a queue at the telephone-company office to place a call, only to have the village's diesel-generated power supply fail as I handed the number to the operator. Caused by generator malfunction or a deliberate shutdown gauged to conserve diesel fuel until the next supply ship puts into port, power outages are an all-too-common occurrence in Puerto Ayora.

One evening, over a ham radio belonging to our neighbours Patricia and Jorgé Valdivieso, I tried to contact friends in the Ecuadorian village of Cumbaya, 800 miles to the east, high in the Andes Mountains. By calling Jorgé's father in Quito on the radio, we were able to patch into the telephone system and dial our friends Helen and Charles Hornby, a retired American couple who have lived in South America for years. Fighting to make my message heard through the static on the radio, I explained my equipment failure to Charles. He, in turn, sent a telex to my father-in-law, Des Clements, in Toronto, asking for replacements. Three weeks later, I received the strobes via tour guides of the California-based Wilderness Travel — after paying the company a rather larcenous $200 (U.S.) delivery fee.

Despite a few such expensive favours, I found that the islands' isolation usually inspired a generous spirit in people. One over-

Frans Lanting

loaded CBC film producer, Nancy Archibald, on assignment for *The Nature of Things*, agreed to take a small package of film back to Toronto for me. This was a godsend, for I had no other means of sending exposed film to Canada for processing. Not trusting the postal service, I had few opportunities to ship film home so that my father-in-law could monitor the progress of my shoot. Although I was able to check the performance of my equipment periodically using black-and-white film that I could develop myself in the islands, I needed Des to check my colour slides for any irregularities in film or equipment.

It was a busy two days in port, but with strobes coming one way and film going the other, I was ready for another expedition. I loaded my gear on the *Normita*, and at 3:30 a.m., we weighed anchor and set a westward course out of Academy Bay for southern Isla Isabela. It was May 26, two months to the day since I had off-loaded my crates from the hold of the *Bucanero*. On this, our second expedition, we had a new captain and cook on board, as our original captain was ill and Jorgé had not been

Volcanic cliffs fall away to the sea at Punta Vincente Roca on the northwest tip of Isla Isabela. Offshore, the Cromwell Current rises to the surface, producing the coldest seawater temperatures of the Galápagos.

Just as they have for half a billion years, sponges, one of the most primitive of multicelled animals, spread over the subtidal landscape, adding a brilliant touch of colour to everything they adorn.

A community of flowerlike
zoanthid anemones, each the size
of a human's little finger,
surrounds a growth of hard
coralline algae.

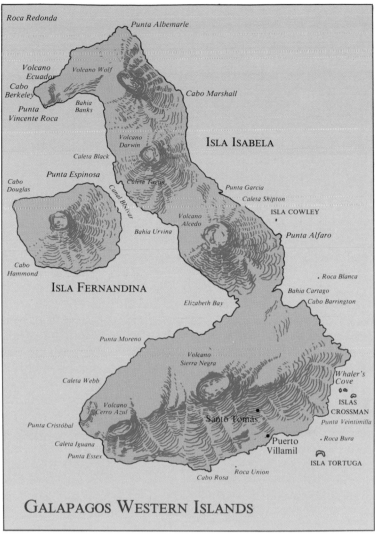

GALAPAGOS WESTERN ISLANDS

impressed with the unimaginative fare that Juan had cooked during the first trip. Our new captain, Lacturo, suffered from failing vision, a distinct disadvantage that added some comic relief during the voyage and was a clear indication of my limited budget. On the other hand, Eduardo, our young cook, excelled at whipping up an endless assortment of unusual but delicious seafood entrées. Jorgé, our guide Mario Possa (who was available to rejoin us when another job was cancelled) and biologist Jack Grove rounded out our crew.

Jack, an American in his mid-thirties, had a week off from his job as chief naturalist aboard the *Bucanero*. With a shaved head, full beard and muscular physique, he looks every bit a sailor. Jack has traversed most of the world's oceans and has spent more than seven years travelling through the Galápagos Islands, diving when and where he can, taking pictures and collecting specimens for biological research. I was fortunate to have him along, for few people are as knowledgeable about the marine life of the Galápagos as he.

Geographically, the western sector of the archipelago encompasses Isla Fernandina and the huge island of Isabela. At 72 miles long by 52 miles at its widest, Isla Isabela constitutes more than half the landmass of the Galápagos Islands. Great shield volcanoes form the island's base, making it one of the most active oceanic volcanic regions on the globe. Five of its six major volcanoes are active; only Volcano Ecuador, at the north end of the island, lies dormant.

Isla Isabela was the site of an immense fire that started in March 1985, less than a month after I had left the islands. The blaze consumed 100,000 acres of grassland and forest and burned out of control for a month and a half. The fire was reportedly started by residents of the hamlet of Santo Tomás, on the southern end of the island, when they put a match to some diseased coffee bushes. No rain had fallen for at least eight months, and the seared and arid brush quickly became an uncontrollable inferno. While 1986 reports indicate that tortoises and iguanas fared well enough, birds and plant life were not so lucky. It will take years to determine exactly how much damage the wildlife has sustained, but there is little doubt that it is severe, perhaps to the point of extinction for some species.

Isla Fernandina, which lies to the west of Isabela, is an island dominated by a single large and active volcano. It is the youngest island in the Galápagos group, and over the last 150 years, there have been a dozen recorded eruptions, the latest occurring in 1977. Punta Espinosa, the only tourist landing site on the island, has the islands' largest colony of marine iguanas.

To witness just how dramatically the marine community of Isla Fernandina and the west coast of Isla Isabela is shaped by the cool, nutrient-laden waters of the Equatorial Undercurrent, or Cromwell Current, I had planned the trip to take us to the far reaches of the western marine province. By boat, the distance from Puerto Ayora to Punta Espinosa is roughly 130 miles, and in the *Normita*, that meant a lot of steaming.

As we travelled west from Isla Santa Cruz, I went below and caught a couple of hours of sleep, lulled by the gentle rhythm of low southwesterly swells. When I climbed back on deck in the dim light of morning, the silhouette of Isla Isabela lay off to starboard, and I could just define the shadowy arc of Islas Crossman. My itinerary for that day included dives there and at Isla Tortuga to the southwest.

A chart of the waters surrounding Islas Crossman indicates a sharp drop just offshore of 400 to 500 feet, and I fully expected

A three-inch-diameter brittle-star (*Ophiotrix* sp), its arms bristling with feeding "hairs" that filter plankton, moves across a forest of black coral (*Antipathes panamensis*). If seized by one of its arms, it will shed the appendage to escape.

to find a rich aggregation of marine life there. We opted to dive the north face of the easternmost island in the group. The Zodiac was chock-full of tanks and regulators, underwater cameras and strobes as Jorgé steered Mario, Jack and me toward the base of an 80-foot cliff. We were so anxious to get into the water that we nearly pushed each other overboard in our struggle to strap on tanks and pull on flippers within the confines of the 14-foot inflatable boat.

Almost as one, we hit the water, making a deafening splash in the surrounding silence. Jorgé handed my camera housings over the side of the boat, and Mario, Jack and I drifted slowly toward the rock face, 15 feet away. I steadied myself against the rocks by grasping the wall like a submarine mountain climber free of ropes and crampons, my depth controlled simply by the push of a button to regulate the air in my flotation device. I switched on my strobes, and we worked our way west along the cliff against a slight current.

I nuzzled into a vertical crack with just enough room to po-

sition the camera. As I had anticipated, the rocks were awash with yellow and red cup corals, blue and lavender sponges, bright, colourful anemones and feathery tube worms. Splayed atop a tennis-ball-sized lavender sponge lay a brittle-star, a tiny sea star with a central disc slightly smaller than a dime from which five 4-inch-long snakelike arms radiate. These arms are shed at the slightest provocation, hence the name brittle-star. As the sponge pumped water through its body to extract food particles, the brittle-star sat atop the stream of exhaust water and fed on the leftovers.

The tiny claws of a white-and-red-banded shrimp nipped repeatedly at creatures invisible to me. This barber-pole shrimp is normally busy cleaning parasites from fish that are attracted to it by its long white antennae. This particular species of shrimp usually works at night and specializes in the grooming of moray eels.

I watched as a bug-eyed goby, nearly transparent save for fine neon-blue stripes running along its 1½-inch-long body,

A golden-phase guineafowl pufferfish (*Arothron meleagris*) emerges cautiously from a shallow crevice. Most predators avoid the pufferfish because of its toxic skin, but when approached, the puffer simply inflates itself.

Within seconds, this pufferfish grew to three times its normal size. It went from a football shape to that of a basketball, making it unmanageable to all but the largest fish.

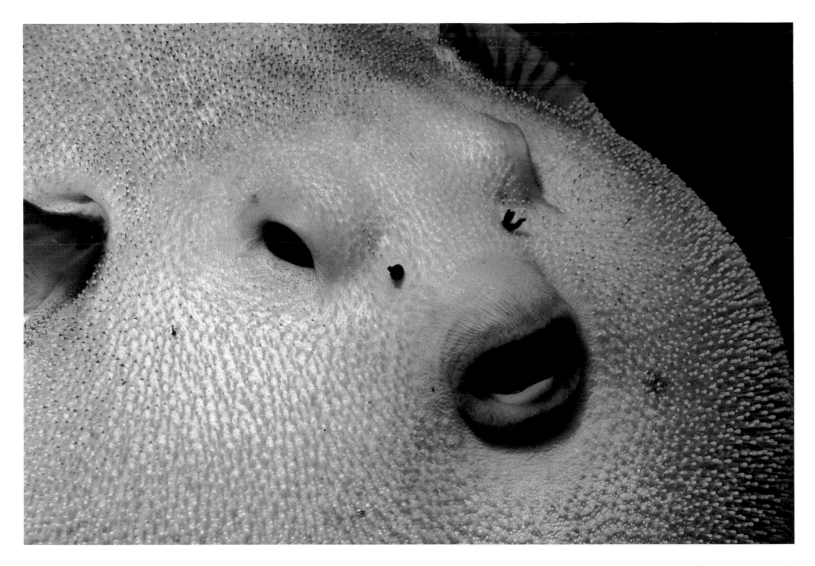

cautiously emerged from its hideout. It waited placidly at the mouth of its den, darting out periodically to nab microscopic plankton. Every time the goby rushed out to feed, the tube worms surrounding its tiny cave instantly withdrew into their calcareous tubes. After the goby returned to its perch, the tube worms would slowly reappear, looking remarkably like a bouquet of spring flowers.

Mario tapped me on the leg; in his hand was a spiny yellow ball—a pufferfish. These fish are normally oblong in shape, but when disturbed, they inflate themselves by gulping water to look menacing and less appealing to eat. There are several species of puffers, but I had never seen one quite so round. One more gulp, and I am sure it would have burst. Mario released his captive, and shortly thereafter, I spotted a banded-tail surgeonfish, an Indo-Pacific species that is common in the northern islands but rare to the south. The presence of the banded-tail surgeonfish at Islas Crossman is a lesson in the way nature abhors absolutes. Although the Galápagos marine environment is scien-

tifically divided into four distinct provinces, there are no submarine walls to prevent the movement of animals from one area to another.

Forty minutes into the dive, we reached the northwest tip of the island and shallower water. What had begun as a sheer drop-off had risen to a flat plain 35 feet below the surface. We were swimming over solid ground, rather than an abyss, and we could see the bottom trailing gently out to sea. I sighted a seven-foot white-tip shark resting beneath a large overhang in 15 to 20 feet of water. I tried to move in closer but had trouble making headway against a strong surge. Diving in the shallows when the surf is up is somewhat like being on an underwater swing: one moment the water pushes you forward, in the next it whisks you back to where you started. If the seafloor is smooth (and one is not prone to seasickness), it can actually be entertaining to drift to and fro with the flow of the water. However, if the bottom is not so smooth, a diver is in danger of being battered against the jagged rocks—a problem I had to contend with.

Stretched to the point of explosion, the pufferfish could hardly swim. I had never seen a puffer so bloated and took advantage of its helplessness to get a close look at its unusual face.

A colony of tube worms (family
Serpulidae) flourishes on a palette
of purple coralline algae. Free-
swimming at birth, tube worms
eventually cement their heads to a
rocky substrate and fabricate a
calcareous tube in which to live.

In a setting reminiscent of more
northerly waters off California,
coralline red algae flourish among
strands of kelp. Despite the fact
that it is so close to the equator,
the west coast of Isla Isabela is
affected by cold-water currents.

component of the zooplankton consumed by baleen whales.

Hundreds upon hundreds of creolefish swam about us during the dive. As if punched from the same mould, they seemed identical, like fish patterned on wallpaper. Schooling fish tend to sort themselves according to size, because larger individuals are faster than smaller fish of the same species and the school must move as a unit. We encountered schools on almost every dive: angelfish, grunts, butterflyfish, tunas, groupers, wrasses and even hammerhead sharks, swimming in uniform, coordinated packs of a few dozen to several hundred members. Why they school is a mystery. Some scientists say that it is for protection, yet the hammerhead shark hardly needs such a safeguard; others speculate that reproduction may be enhanced when eggs and sperm are shed into the water, but some schools are composed of only one sex. Regardless, the schools added a touch of excitement to our underwater observations.

It became increasingly difficult to photograph the wealth of marine life as water conditions deteriorated. Even 50 feet below the surface, the powerful surge could push me about. I steadied myself as best I could by wrapping legs and arms around anything solid but was scarcely able to keep still long enough to release the camera shutter. The constant struggle to remain motionless was exhausting; so, frustrated after only 40 minutes underwater, I signalled Jack and Mario that it was time to call it quits.

My original plan had been to sail the long and windswept shoreline of southern Isla Isabela, around Punta Cristóbal, then to drive as far north as possible along the west coast before nightfall; but with the seas running five and six feet out of the south, we altered our course and opted for the protected passage afforded by the eastern shore. Before heading north, we had to sail in an easterly direction, which left us broadside to the southern swells. The *Normita* bobbed as wave crests poured into troughs, and the gunwales dipped dangerously close to the sea. We endured an hour of being tossed about before setting stern to the restless sea — an hour that confirmed our decision to abandon the southern route.

Bahia Cartago was our planned anchorage for the night, but it would be many hours before we reached our goal in the slow-moving *Normita*, even with the help of a trailing sea. With the swells running from behind, the *Normita*'s pitching and rolling was less erratic, and I was able to catch up on some much-needed sleep. When I awoke from my afternoon nap, I went topside and settled into my favourite spot at the bow, where I could collect my thoughts and marvel at the contorted landscape of barren black lava.

Fifteen million years ago, there was a faint hiss as molten lava shot through the Earth's crust into the Pacific Ocean. Even if humans had been on the planet, they would not have heard a thing, for this occurred hundreds of miles from land and thousands of yards beneath the surface of the sea. In the womb of what is now called the Galápagos Platform, the Galápagos Islands were conceived. Amid the turmoil of a planet in the throes of geological evolution, this eruption was hardly remarkable. And it was not an isolated event but one that recurred over the millennia.

During a 12-million-year gestation, volcanic eruptions on the ocean floor forced more and more magma into the sea where, upon meeting the cold water, it cooled instantaneously and drifted to the bottom. With each eruption, the lava mass drew closer to the surface. Three to five million years ago, Earth celebrated the birth of new islands. The area around Baltra and northern Santa Cruz was pushed above sea level. Isla Isabela, which I was scanning from my perch, broke the surface many years later. Because it is a much younger island than Baltra or Santa Cruz, it is still volcanically active.

We reached Bahia Cartago without incident and passed a quiet night there. I awoke at 5:30 a.m. to the sound of waves lapping gently against the hull. Topside, the sky was spectacular. As the sun rose, the horizon was bathed in a deep burnt orange that changed over the next several minutes to consecutively paler tints, as if an indecisive artist had at first chosen the deepest shade of orange, then continually washed it to produce lighter and lighter hues.

By 7 a.m., we were on our way toward the small island of Cowley, and a few hours later, we rounded the north side of the island. While Mario, Jack and I were loading equipment into the Zodiac, the captain took time out for some fishing, hauling in a 25-pound amberjack, which was followed almost immediately by two more. After we entered the water, the reason for such good fishing became evident: we were surrounded by a school of three-foot amberjacks. The way these large, spirited fish swam around us, often close enough to touch, was enchanting. At times, 50 to 60 fish would swim directly toward me, only to split into two groups, one passing on each side. I felt like a rock in the middle of a stream of fish. At one point, I lunged at a fish in a playful attempt to grab its tail and hitch a ride. Instead of being spooked, the fish turned around at once and adopted a threatening posture. For the rest of the dive, I assumed a look-but-don't-touch philosophy with the amberjacks.

Upon descending, I was disappointed to find that very few invertebrates had taken refuge among the scattered boulders; presumably, there was insufficient water movement along this sheltered side to provide enough food for extensive benthic life. The dive was not altogether boring, however. I was able to catch a very large porcupinefish that had backed itself into a shallow cave formed by two large boulders. I eased it out of the crevice and held it gently in my hands while it inflated itself by gulping large quantities of water. It was round and about the size of a soccer ball by the time it had finished. Jack wanted to take its picture, so I jokingly stuck it under my arm like a football and started petting its head, at which point it opened its mouth in what can only be described as a grin. When I stopped petting, it ceased grinning. Stroking resumed, another grin. I finally had to release it because I was laughing so hard that I flooded my mask.

After the dive, the captain fished for about half an hour before I could coax him to get under way. I had a strict policy of no fishing while anyone was in the water, in case sharks became frenzied at the erratic movements of a fish struggling on the end of a line. To the locals, however, fish mean money, and since we had a freezer on board, the captain was bent on catching enough for us to eat during our trip plus some to sell when we returned to port. I am sure the captain would have preferred to remain there fishing, rather than ferrying us around, but we had a long journey ahead, and I was anxious to reach the west coast of Isla Isabela.

The captain was a practical man to whom scuba diving made little sense. While he was happy enough for this job, he was hardly attuned to what we were doing. Plagued by cockroaches one day, he took an aerosol can of insecticide to the two-inch pests, spraying everything in sight, including the intake hose for my air compressor. Luckily, I caught him and explained as best I could with my Spanish and hand gestures the consequences of breathing insecticide that finds its way into our tanks through the compressor. With a shrug, he promised not to spray my equipment again and returned to the tiller, leaving me to clean out the intake hose.

We were hoping to round Punta Albemarle, at the northeastern tip of Isabela, before sundown, but the distance was too great and the *Normita* too slow, despite the continued heavy trailing sea. We managed to reach Cabo Marshall by 4 p.m. and

decided to make another daylight dive at the first sheltered spot we found. It was while pulling into a little bay to anchor that our captain received a nickname that lasted well past the end of the trip. In fairness, Lacturo knew the waters well, but the years were taking their toll on his eyesight; to compensate for his failing vision, he was always extremely cautious when close to land. Any manoeuvring within about a mile of solid ground was done at half-throttle, which, for the *Normita*, was equivalent to a leisurely backstroke. Since this was all new ground to me, I was happy that the captain tended to err on the careful side; however, Jack and Mario, who both knew the area, were almost driven to mutiny.

We crept into the cove with Jack and Mario directing from the bow. They urged the captain to move closer to shore so we could benefit from the shelter provided by the coast. The captain shook his head, shouting, "*Franja, franja!*" (There's a shelf, there's a shelf!), and ordered them to drop anchor. Once the anchor was set and the *Normita* had swung around at the end of the rope in

sympathy with the current, we were too close to yet another *franja*, and we had to raise the anchor and try another spot. It was almost dark by the time we finally anchored and were suited up, and tempers were high. After this, Jack and I avoided the hassles of anchoring by jumping into the Zodiac to pass the time fishing and left the mooring to "Captain Franja" and his crew.

By 5:30 the following morning, we were on the way to our next planned dive at Punta Albemarle. The winds had remained brisk during the night, and the sea was still heavy out of the south. We were a few days shy of June, and the Galápagos Islands were entering the *garúa* season, when the trade winds prevail out of the southeast and push the cool waters of the Peru Current system into the archipelago. This change often brings unsettled weather, stronger winds and rougher seas.

That morning, we crossed the equator into the northern hemisphere. We rounded Punta Albemarle, leaving behind the lengthy east-coast passage. The seas changed from rolling to rippled as we travelled the lee side of the north coast of Isla Isabela. I noticed

Schools of surgeonfish (*Prionurus laticlavius*), named for the scalpel-sharp spine at the base of the tail, are a common sight over shallow-water reefs where their only food, algae, is most abundant.

an old building and the remains of a transmitter tower on shore. During World War II, the U.S. military had established a communications station there. We anchored in a sheltered cove west of that desolate spot.

I was itching to dive, for we were now on the fringe of an area where the underwater ecology is noticeably shaped by the Cromwell Current. We ran the Zodiac to within 40 feet of the shore at the western point of the tiny bay where huge boulders dot the coast. I was the first one into the water, and 30 seconds later, I wanted to be the first one to get out. Cold 64-degree (F) water trickled down my back, leaving goose bumps in its path. My wet suit slowly filled with seawater that felt so cold, I imagined myself diving in more northerly waters off the coast of California.

The underwater scenery differed drastically from that of previous dives. Algae grew ubiquitously upon the rocky seafloor: broad seersucker leaves of greens and browns; large bundles of narrow strands clustered like dunegrass on a sandy shore; and short tufts cropped closely atop the many boulders. Some warmwater corals were also present, living at what must have been the limit of their tolerance for the cold. It was an incongruous blend of flora and fauna. We spent 50 minutes exploring the caverns and caves before surfacing. I was shivering when I left the water and put on several layers of clothing to get warm — ironic, given that I was but a few miles north of the equator.

The Pacific Ocean proved as tranquil as its name as we motored across the northern coast of Isabela. I was standing at the bow gazing northwestward toward Roca Redonda when a sizable whale surfaced, spouting a misty plume. Too distant to identify, it disappeared beneath the surface, abandoning us to the loneliness of the western sector of the Galápagos archipelago.

We rounded Cabo Berkeley shortly after noon. I had expected to encounter a choppy sea, since the western side of Isla Isabela is largely exposed to the full force of the vast Pacific Ocean. Instead, it remained calm. The water looked so clear and the sun's rays penetrated so deeply that I fancied I could see the bottom, and Jack remarked that he had seldom seen conditions so favourable there. Captain Franja grudgingly consented to move closer to shore, and not far past Cabo Berkeley, we sighted two caves gouged out of the cliff face that plunged into the sea. Jack had noticed the caves in his travels, but neither time nor sea conditions had ever cooperated to allow him to dive there. We decided to seize the opportunity.

A glint of light a few hundred yards out to sea caught my eye as I boarded the Zodiac. I was straining to see its source when a dolphin leapt from the water and, for an instant, hung motionless 10 feet above the surface before dropping back into the sea. Then another leapt, and still another, as the pod bounded toward us. We sped a short distance from the *Normita* in the Zodiac until the dolphins surrounded us. I jumped into the clear water for a closer view of their spectacular performance. With stunning

Confused by the bright colours of reef fish such as this wrasse (*Bodianus diplotaenia*), predators may have trouble distinguishing their prey from the vividly coloured invertebrates on the reef.

Lacy strands of red algae cling to the seafloor by means of primitive roots, called holdfasts, that allow the algae to withstand the constant tug of ocean currents.

A pod of playful, squeaking
bottlenose dolphins (*Tursiops
truncatus*) joined Mario, Jack and
me for half an hour near Cabo
Berkeley, executing a series of
somersaults before leaving as
suddenly as they had appeared.

speed, they would rocket to the surface and vault into the air, hang in suspended animation against the sky, then plummet back into the sea. It was a novelty to see the flip side of a dolphin's leap.

The revue continued for more than half an hour without a break in tempo, all the while accompanied by an uninterrupted dialogue of high-pitched squeaks and clicks. With no sense of smell to help locate food or enemies, the dolphin relics on echolocation. By sending out sound signals until they strike an object and return to its large and complex brain (most probably through its jaw and throat), a dolphin can compute an object's direction, distance, speed, size and configuration.

Long before I had had enough, the dolphins dispersed, their voices lingering after they had disappeared from sight. In all the excitement, I had drained my scuba tank, even though I was never more than 50 feet deep and was underwater less than 45 minutes. During a relaxed dive at that depth, I could have stretched the air supply in my 72-cubic-foot tank to last an hour and a half. So, rather than going straight to the caves for our dive, we had

to return to the *Normita* to refill our cylinders and reload our cameras. That accomplished, we piled into the Zodiac again and moved closer to shore with the intention of exploring the caves. Despite the calm conditions on the surface, however, there was still sufficient swell action to prevent us from safely entering the shallow-water caverns. Instead, we swam away from the shore where the motion was not as bothersome.

The seafloor consisted of huge boulders into which were carved narrow channels and deep horizontal crevices. Algae formed mosaics of greens, golds, oranges and blues on any surface that sunlight could reach; the water was so clear that the colours, usually muted at 40 to 50 feet, were vibrant. The seaweeds and grasses swayed in sympathy with the swell action, a marine ballet of incomparable grace. I landed on my knees on a white sandy strip, six feet away from a horned shark; it was about three feet long, light with darker spots, and blended in quite well with the bottom. I sprawled onto my stomach and inched nearer to photograph its face close up. The eyes were typically sharklike, hollow

While many fish roam the sea in search of prey, most groupers, such as this *Dermatolepis dermatolepis*, hide in a suitable crevice or cave and suck in unwitting victims passing within range of their powerful mouths.

time capsules leading back millions of years; the mouth looked as if it had been caught in a shredder, with fat fleshy appendages that resembled stumpy fingers rather than lips. The grotesque mouth is designed to allow the shark to move sand and debris effectively as it scours the seafloor for animals, such as shellfish, to eat.

When I had moved too close, the horned shark finned 20 feet away and once again settled on the bottom. I swam after it until I noticed a coil of delicate pink strands lying on a bed of brown algae. Nearby, amidst dense kelp, were several tan jellylike creatures, which I recognized as sea hares. There, gathered in a courtship ritual, were five or six of these shell-less mollusks, varying in size from 8 to 10 inches long. Like their cousin the octopus, sea hares can change their colour to match their surroundings, and here, they blended in with the brown algae, busy with the drive to reproduce. A stringy mass of pink eggs lay beside the sea hares like a pile of wool from an unravelled sweater. Close by, several huddles of sea hares were busy laying eggs. Adding further colour to a fascinating dive were huge aggregates of golf-ball-sized anemones that carpeted the rocks just below the surface; many damselfish, blennies and gobies; several sea turtles; and the occasional sea ray on the sand. The dive had a special significance, for I knew that few people, if any, had ever dived this often inaccessible site.

We left the caves south of Cabo Berkeley and continued down the coast toward Punta Vincente Roca, where we planned to spend the night. From the northern approach, a large bay lies concealed behind Punta Vincente Roca. The setting of the cove is a wonder to behold: precipitous cliffs spill into the sea, their flanks a testimony to the massive forces that pushed millions of tons of solid rock above sea level. I took the Zodiac, combining a bit of fishing with a tour of the bluffs. A close examination revealed distinct striations marking successive lava flows. The fishing was great along the eastern shore of the bay, and I soon had enough grouper for our evening meal.

After supper, Jack and I prepared for a night dive, the first one I would make in the Galápagos Islands. Diving at night is a unique experience; the excitement lies in its simplicity. Enveloped in a shroud of darkness, a diver must focus and concentrate on whatever the light illuminates. Creatures caught momentarily in the beam are like undersea fireflies. Many marine creatures are nocturnal, and the only time they can be seen is at night. As well, behaviour patterns change. For example, fish that are often impossible to approach during the day can almost be touched when mesmerized by the light; others assume different colour patterns.

We headed to the extreme northwest side of the bay to a cave 30 to 40 feet across at the mouth and high enough to accommodate an adult standing up in a boat. At the entrance, I gazed upward to see the stars blazing brightly in the nearly moonless sky. Mario steered us into the ink-black cave, where Jack and I eased

A harmless three-foot-long horned shark (*Heterodontus quoyi*) lies motionless on the seafloor. Its camouflage colouring is typical of many bottom feeders that almost disappear into their surroundings.

ourselves into the water and began sinking to the bottom. I switched on my dive light, and the cave wall erupted in brilliant hues of orange, red and yellow as the beam danced over sponges and corals. I worked my way deeper into the cave and saw a dazzling red spotted hawkfish that would have been mostly white during the day.

After 45 minutes, Jack's light was all but spent, and we were both shivering from the 62-degree water. We returned to the surface where Mario was waiting for us in the Zodiac. I handed him my camera, scuba tank and weight belt and floated on the surface, buoyed by my wet suit. I drifted slightly away from the boat and stared at the heavens; the stars appeared brighter than when we had started our dive. I thought about the possibility of following the cave through the cliff into the saltwater lake inland, which is no doubt possible because sea lions often frequent the lake. But an undertaking of that sort would require extra scuba tanks, regulators, rope and other special equipment that we did not have with us.

Jack and I decided we would dive the outside of Punta Vincente Roca in the morning. Since leaving Puerto Ayora, we had endured long passages that often began before daybreak to compensate for the *Normita*'s lack of speed. So we decided to sleep late the following day.

Over breakfast that fourth morning, Jorgé informed me that we had only half a tank of fuel left. We still had not reached the halfway point of our journey, so a lengthy discussion ensued to determine how we were going to proceed. In the end, we agreed to continue down the west coast of Isabela and around the southern tip, hoping to reach the village of Puerto Villamil before we ran out of diesel fuel. I had two concerns: first, since we had no radio, if we happened to run out of fuel before reaching Puerto Villamil, it could be a long time before someone found us because only a few of the larger and faster charter boats use that route; second, there was no guarantee of fuel in Puerto Villamil, which could mean a week or two of waiting for a supply ship. We had already had difficulty securing fuel in Puerto Ayora, and a shortage in Puerto Villamil would bring our diving to a standstill. We could only pray that a supply ship with diesel fuel would beat us to Puerto Villamil.

The decision made, Jack, Mario and I raced out to Punta Vincente Roca for a dive. Even before we had jumped into the water, it was apparent that the water conditions had changed for the worse, and we could hardly see beneath the surface. I rolled into

the sea but found it difficult to orient myself. The water was the colour of pea soup, and visibility was zero. The Cromwell Current was showing its stuff: the nutrient-rich water that had welled up to the surface as it reached the coast of Isabela had spawned a massive bloom of phytoplankton.

Diatoms and dinoflagellates—microscopic plant plankton at the base of the food web—are tiny ocean drifters found in all seas of the world. Under conditions of strong sunlight and abundant nutrients such as nitrates and phosphates, phytoplankton reproduce at an astounding rate. Some, like the dinoflagellates, have short life cycles that amount to only a few hours. But in that brief time, a cubic foot of water can spawn millions of these tiny plants, each containing chlorophyll-rich cells that impart a greenish hue to seawater.

Plankton, in high concentrations, is the bane of underwater photographers: visibility is reduced, and picture taking becomes an almost fruitless exercise. Still, we descended farther to try to get below the "plankton layer." At 40 feet, the visibility improved marginally, but it remained poor even down to 100 feet. I had waited impatiently for the opportunity to dive the western marine province, and I was sorely vexed by the turn of events.

The dive did prove of value to Jack, however, because it answered one of his many questions concerning the El Niño, a weather disturbance in 1982-83 that had wreaked havoc on the Galápagos archipelago as well as on five continents. The El Niño

93

The jaws of the horned shark (*Heterodontus quoyi*) are rimmed with fat, fleshy appendages that move sand and debris during the shark's search for mollusks and crustaceans.

A shell-less mollusk with male and
female reproductive organs, the
sea hare (*Aplysia* sp) lays millions
of eggs in a lifetime. Sea hares
participate in a mass-fertilization
ritual before setting off alone to
deposit their eggs on the seabed.

occurs at irregular intervals — sometimes two years apart, other times as many as 10 years apart — and its roots lie in a reversal of pressure systems in the South Pacific that causes the easterly trade winds to falter. The easterlies are replaced by westerly winds that force the surface currents to reverse and start warm water flowing toward South America. The force of the 1982-83 El Niño was so strong that oceanic temperature changes were felt as far north as British Columbia. Fishermen throughout the Pacific Northwest were catching species that did not belong there, and they could not find those that did. It damaged the fisheries, inflicting a severe blow on an already fragile industry. Even more pronounced were the droughts it caused in places as far-flung as Australia and Ethiopia and the floods it precipitated in countries such as Ecuador and Peru. Before the El Niño ended in 1983, more than 1,100 people had died as a result of it, and damage was estimated at $8.7 billion (U.S.).

In the Galápagos Islands, water temperatures began to rise in the early part of 1982. By August 1983, according to Jack, sea-surface temperatures were recorded in excess of 86 degrees. The changes this brought about were phenomenal. As the warm waters converged on the archipelago from the north and west, upwelling ceased, natural marine productivity levels dropped, and the oceanographic parameters that normally define the four distinct marine provinces became meaningless. As water temperatures rose, those creatures that could migrate, such as many of the larger fish, moved to deeper water or out of the islands altogether. But animals such as corals and other invertebrates and most smaller fish were incapable of such movement and perished en masse.

The rusty damselfish (*Nexilosus latifrons*) is one fish that was trapped. It had not been seen since the El Niño and was thought by some to have disappeared entirely. Little wonder, then, that Jack was ecstatic upon surfacing from what I had considered a lousy dive: he had sighted a rusty damselfish for the first time since the El Niño.

In light of the decreased visibility that morning, we supposed that the rest of the west coast would be equally poor for diving. Rather than face the frustration of murky waters and given the uncertainty of our fuel supply, I directed the captain to retrace our course via the northern route to Isla Santa Cruz. I regretted having to abandon the western reaches of the archipelago, for it was there, during my trip aboard the *Bucanero*, that I had watched a vigorous game of "iguana toss" between two sea lions.

At the time, I was land-bound on a sandy beach on a point near our landing site, and I had returned for a closer look at both the sea lions and the marine iguanas. As I watched, a sea lion, coming up from underneath, grasped an iguana in its mouth, swam underwater a short distance, then rose to the surface and flung the helpless lizard into the air. No sooner had the iguana hit the water and started to swim toward shore than another sea lion repeated the game, sending the iguana back in the direction of the first sea lion. This was repeated several times until the sea lions were bored. When the hapless iguana finally reached the safety of terra firma, it sprawled in the sun, seeming none the worse for wear.

Marine iguanas (*Amblyrhynchus cristatus*) are an anomaly in that they are the only lizard known to take to the sea regularly to feed. At low tide, they eat the seaweeds and algae that cover the rocks and will dive as deep as 35 feet to graze on plants. They can stay submerged for a considerable length of time, as a sailor with biologist Charles Darwin proved in 1835 when he tied a heavy rock around a lizard and left it on the ocean bottom, retrieving it, still alive, an hour later.

Sadly, though, the marine iguanas of Punta Espinosa would not be on my agenda this time. Pushing northward, we passed Cabo Berkeley and began to swing around the point and on across the top of Isla Isabela. Almost as if a hidden wall separated the two, the dark green pea soup changed to bluish green, and visibility improved markedly.

The whitestripe chromis (*Chromis alta*), the Galápagos' only deep-water damselfish, seldom swims alone. I spotted this one in front of a gorgonian coral.

In the early afternoon, we lashed down all equipment on board in preparation for rounding the northeast corner of Isla Isabela and steaming southward. We pushed forward against a choppy sea and finally dropped anchor just north of Cabo Marshall. At 2:30 the next morning, we set out through a black sea illuminated by what looked like a million stars. Our destination was Isla Santiago. Wrapped in warm clothes, I stood at the bow and watched a faint light on the horizon. Another boat was making its way south, its handful of passengers sharing with us the night magic of the Galápagos Islands.

Later that morning, we dived Isla Albany off the north shore of Isla Santiago, then Buccaneer Cove on Santiago itself. Both dives were disappointing, revealing only silty bottoms dotted very infrequently with drab invertebrates. The contrast between these sites in the central marine province and those along the west coast of Isabela in the western sector illustrates the importance of plankton. In the vicinity of Isla Santiago, where there is little upwelling to bring nutrients from the depths to support plankton growth, invertebrates must depend on other currents to transport the floating plants and animals to them. When such currents are weak, as they are at the northern end of Isla Santiago, few bottom dwellers can survive.

We anchored in the cove at noon at the popular tourist site of south James Bay on the west coast of Isla Santiago, and I faced another obstacle. While I was filling the scuba tanks en route from Buccaneer Cove, the drive belt on my compressor had split, and I had no spare. We would have to end our trip early if I could not improvise.

Mario and the captain inquired at the *Bronzewing*, a small tourist boat anchored nearby, and returned with two drive belts, both of which were too big. Nevertheless, they *were* drive belts, and we set about modifying the compressor to accept the smaller of the two. Twenty feet of line, two Vise-Grips and three bloodied knuckles later, the compressor was jury-rigged to pump our tanks full of clean high-pressure air.

Along the coast just south of James Bay, there is a series of grottoes carved out of the lava coast whose natural pools and bridges form an aquarium-like setting for Galápagos marine life. The most famous inhabitants are the Galápagos fur seals (*Arctocephalus galapagoensis*) that can be found taking advantage of the grottoes to seek shade from the blazing sun. Their aversion to heat and intense light is not surprising, for they are closely related to the southern fur seal (*A. australis*) that lives in islands

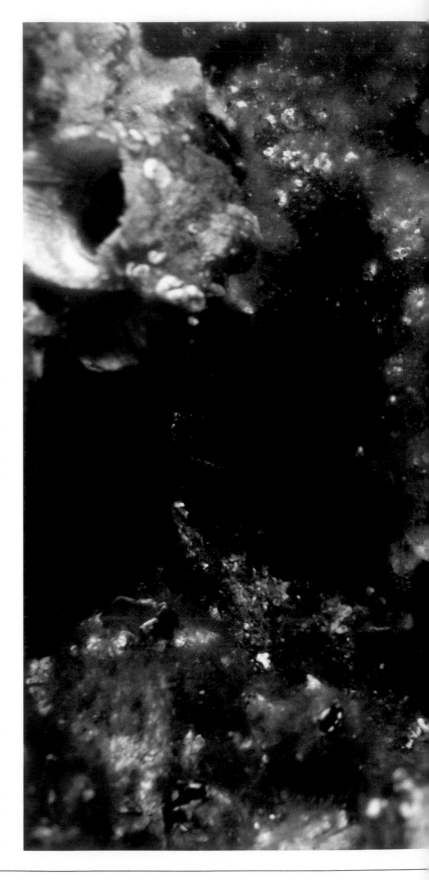

One of the joys of diving at night is the discovery of new versions of familiar species. This spotted hawkfish (*Cirrhitichthys oxycephalus*) displays nighttime coloration that is the opposite of its daytime pattern.

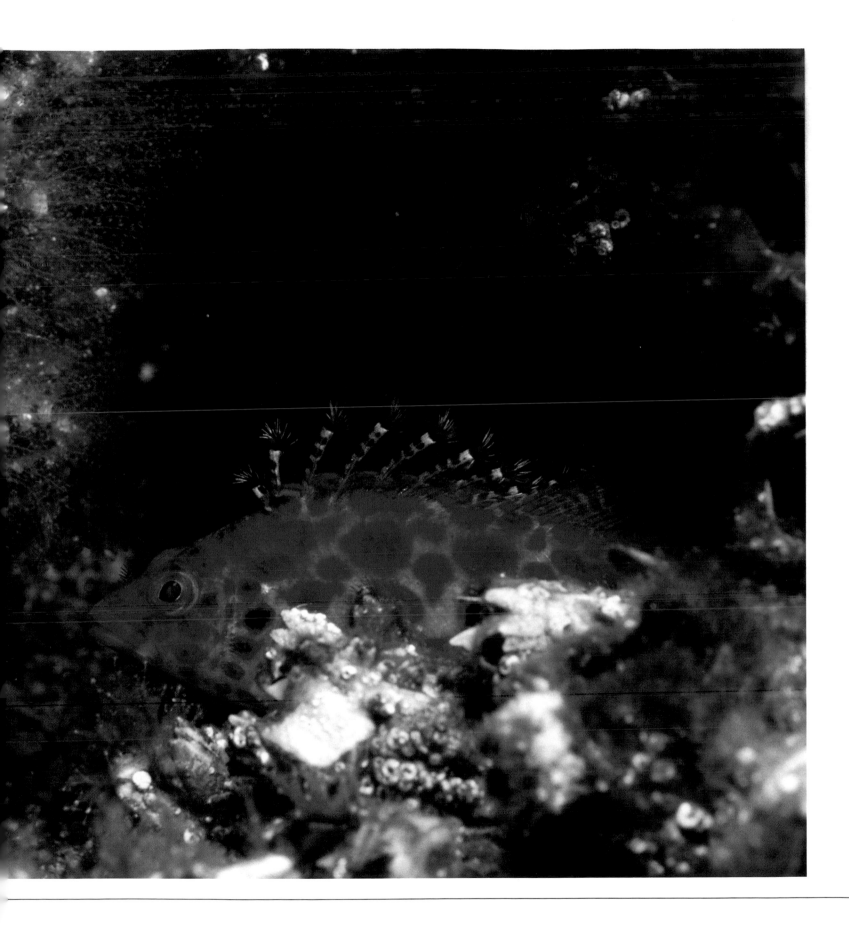

dived into the water and swam rapidly to the mouth of the grotto. Timid as it was, the fur seal did not leave the pool, and I could sense its curiosity building. It was apprehensive when I tried to approach, so I turned my attention to other animals in the pool, with the hope that over time, the seal's confidence would grow and I would be able to photograph it at closer range. My ploy worked, and eventually, it swam nearer. I had just manoeuvred into a position that afforded a better angle from which to take a picture when it turned abruptly and bolted through the pool's entrance and out to sea. I was puzzled by this behaviour until I looked up.

Ringing the top of the pool were eight grotesque silhouettes of human beings. As I exhaled, air bubbles rose to the surface and rippled the quiet pond, which further contorted the figures. They stared at me as if I were a corpse entombed in a watery casket. Until that moment, I had logged hundreds of undisturbed hours underwater, and the vision of these strangers jolted me from my reverie with such force that I struggled to stop shaking.

I was angry as I swam toward the Zodiac, upset that my privacy had been invaded. I had grown so accustomed to enjoying the Galápagos Islands in peace that the human voices I heard as I surfaced beside the Zodiac grated like fingernails drawn across a blackboard. It was then that I realized how precious a companion and assistant Mario was, for he very seldom spoke when we went ashore, preferring not to intrude on the natural sounds of the islands.

Mario helped me into the Zodiac with my gear, then piloted us around the coast to the *Normita*. I looked back and saw the tourists filing in a column along the marked pedestrian path, the park guide stopping the group periodically to point out another wonder of Galápagos nature.

As many as 20,000 people each year choose the Galápagos Islands as their travel destination and tread those paths that the national park service has staked out on many of the major islands. Tourist traffic is controlled so that no area receives more visitors than is healthy for the animal and plant populations, and Miguel Cifuentes, administrator of the Galápagos National Park Service, is to be commended for his dedication to the study and preservation of the flora and fauna of the islands. At present, the park personnel seems to be successfully safeguarding the territory, but if the government of Ecuador were to begin a serious campaign of enticing foreigners — as the democratic government of Léon Febres Cordero has hinted at doing — more trails would have to

near the Antarctic and along the southern coast of South America.

While the fur seals have a luxuriant pelt that keeps them warm, it almost brought about their demise, as they were hunted extensively in the late 18th and early 19th centuries. At one time, their numbers were considered to be dangerously low, but it is now believed that they fared better than was first thought. Their fondness for secretive caves and ledges makes them much less visible than, say, sea lions, and in a population census conducted in 1963, it was estimated that approximately 4,000 Galápagos fur seals inhabited the archipelago.

Mario eased the Zodiac into a tiny inlet that led to a large pool, an impressive rocky archway defining the entrance. The water was crystal-clear, and I could see fish finning past colourful invertebrates scattered along the wall. A fur seal slept peacefully on a ledge toward the back of the pool, and I slipped into the water to swim along the bottom toward it. From my vantage point, I could see the fur seal plainly. Suddenly it awoke, disturbed, perhaps, by air bubbles from my regulator breaking the surface. It

Eduardo, our cook, escaped the confines of the *Normita*'s tiny galley for his washing-up duties. His gastronomic talents and an endless supply of fresh seafood diverted our attention from the cramped quarters.

A Galápagos sea lion (*Zalophus
californianus wollebaeki*) surfaces,
enjoying its freedom to move
between two worlds. I was amazed
at the contrast between the
subtidal world, full of life and
colour, and the parched coast.

A longnose hawkfish (*Oxycirrhites typus*) thoroughly picks over the offerings of a stand of Galápagos black coral (*Antipathes galapagensis*) in its search for microscopic crustaceans.

be cut and more islands would be opened to public intrusion.

Late that afternoon, Jack and Mario went fishing in the Zodiac. After landing a couple of tuna, Jack snagged a shark that swallowed his hook. The shark was much too large to land in the Zodiac, so Mario drove the inflatable up on the beach where, after a considerable struggle, Jack managed to haul the fish ashore. While Jack fought with his catch, Mario returned to the *Normita* to get me. As we neared the shore, I was saddened to see the splendid hunter reduced to a flattened hulk, spasmodically thrashing on the sand. Jack moved quickly to free it from the hook, and together, we guided it back into the water. The experience had greatly weakened the five-foot shark, and although Jack walked with it close to shore to force water through the gills in an attempt to help it breathe, the shark was unable to regain its strength.

We lugged the lifeless shark back onto the beach, where Jack slit its abdomen and extracted eight 10-inch replicas of the mother from the uterus. Each was attached by a pseudo-umbilicus and was perfectly formed except for the lack of teeth. Jack put the tiny sharks into a bucket and, not wanting to leave the carcass to rot on the shore, towed it over to the *Normita* and lashed it to the stern of the boat. Later on, we released it in deeper water, where fish could feed on the sinking flesh. The shark fetuses went into the freezer for Jack to preserve later in formalin.

We dived the fur seal grottoes again the following morning,

then moved on to Islas Beagles, where I had previously encountered clear water and thriving communities of black corals. The water was not as clear as it had been during my last trip through the central islands, but I was still thrilled by the spectacular wall dive that makes Islas Beagles one of my favourite diving locations in the Galápagos. The sea was too rough for the minimal shelter afforded by the cove at Islas Beagles, so we spent the night at Isla Eden, just off the north coast of Santa Cruz. The next morning, we had to abandon our plan to dive Isla Sin Nombre, southeast of Isla Pinzón. Swells from the south were smashing against the steep cliff face of this tiny island, quashing any chance of a dive.

Once again, the time constraints of previous commitments dictated that we return to Puerto Ayora. As we followed the west coast of Isla Santa Cruz, I was entranced by waves pummelling the shore. Scrub brush, cactus and thornbush thrive on this arid land, and beige sandy beaches punctuate the miles of black lava. Had I not known through which of the four sectors of the archipelago I was travelling, the scenery topside would not have resolved my uncertainty. By contrast, I had dived and photographed two marine provinces in the islands and had witnessed firsthand how different each marine community is from the other. My next journey — to the southern islands — would illustrate how the complex system of currents affects yet another region of the Galápagos.

Biologist Jack Grove struggles to resuscitate a five-foot-long shark he hooked while fishing the waters of James Bay, Isla Santiago. The shark had used all its strength fighting the hook, however, and died shortly after.

A quick autopsy on the dead shark revealed eight fetuses in its abdomen. Two weeks too young to survive out of the womb, they were preserved in formalin and used for research.

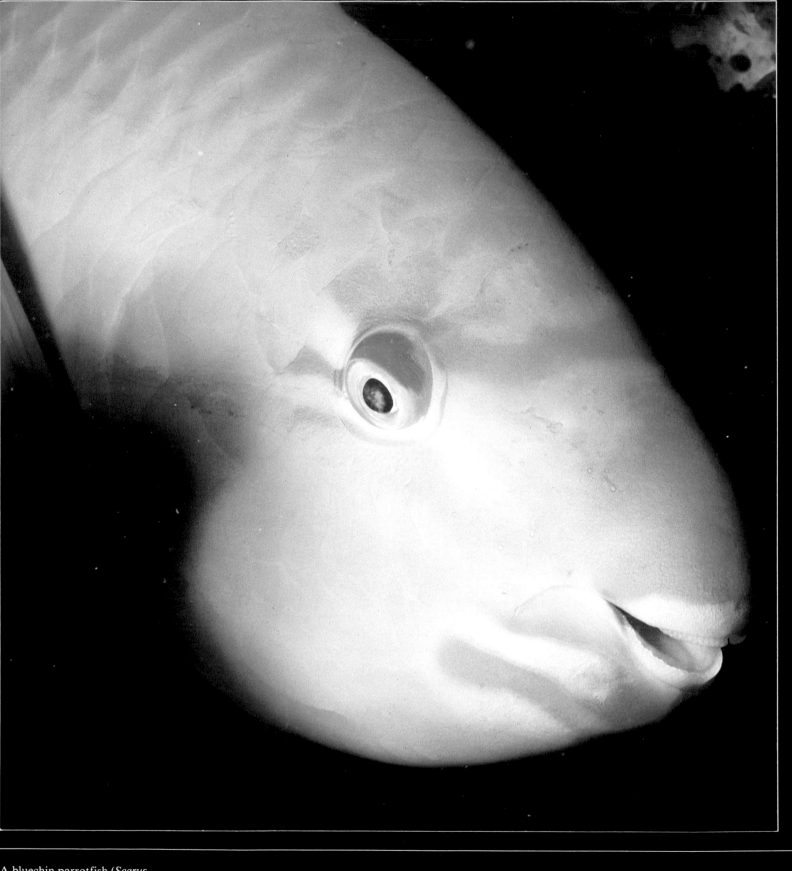

A bluechin parrotfish (*Scarus ghobban*) "sleeps" through one of my nighttime excursions. Despite its alert-looking eyes, the fish will stay in that position until daylight.

Devil's Crown

A southern journey
to shark-infested waters

Slow-moving creatures, such as
this sea urchin (*Eucidaris
thouarsii*), make excellent hosts
for various sorts of marine life.
Only the newest of the spines on
this individual are not encrusted.

Caught in a maelstrom of inquisitive silvery grunts (*Anisotremus interruptus*), I constantly had to shoo this school away from my lens. Mario, extra camera in hand, watched my predicament with amusement.

Sea stars, such as this *Mithrodia bradleyi*, breathe through their skin and would suffocate if they became encrusted with marine organisms. Thus they have evolved an effective array of pincers that keeps them relatively clean.

built his armada near Guayaquil, where balsa wood is plentiful.

The fleet was away at sea for nine months to a year and returned with plunder that included "black people, gold, a brass chair and the skin and jawbone of a horse," most of which was obviously not from the Galápagos Islands. But the skin and jawbone of a horse could, perhaps, have been the remains of a Galápagos sea lion, since horses were not introduced to the New World until 1519. There were also accounts of an "Island of Fire," which could have been one of the volcanically active islands in the group.

The first recorded visit to the Galápagos Islands was in 1535 by Tomás de Berlanga, Bishop of Panama. While sailing southward along the mainland coast toward Peru, his ship was caught in the doldrums and floated for six days until it became trapped in the South Equatorial Current that carried it westward. After riding the current for 10 days, the sailors spotted an island.

The joy of sighting land soured quickly, however, for although a shore party searched several islands for fresh water to replenish their own dangerously low supplies, they found little. They finally discovered a small reservoir of rainwater in a ravine from which they gathered about "eight hogsheads" (approximately 400 imperial gallons) of potable water, but it was hardly enough to satisfy their needs. Theirs was the first of many expeditions that would reach the islands with little or no water and leave without having quenched their thirst. De Berlanga was not impressed with the archipelago. In a letter to Carlos V, Emperor of Spain, he wrote that most of the islands were "full of very big stones, so much so that it seems as though at some time, God had showered stones." He did, however, mention with interest the giant tortoises and the tameness of the birds.

With a meagre supply of water on board, de Berlanga set sail for the mainland, which he assumed was only 60 to 80 miles away. Twenty-one days later, having battled the strong westerly current, the ship had covered 10 times that distance and finally reached Bahia Caráquez on the coast of Ecuador.

The next visitor to the Galápagos Islands was a renegade captain, Diego de Rivadeneira, who had stolen a ship during the civil war in 1546 between Pizarro and the viceroy of Peru. Setting out for New Spain with neither charts nor instruments, his vessel came within sight of land after 25 days at sea. After sailing around the islands for several days, a few men went ashore to find fresh water but returned with nothing more than a few birds. The shore party's exploration had only been cursory, for they had feared that they might be abandoned by the captain. At one point in their voyage, while the ship was becalmed, de Rivadeneira threw a young deckhand into the sea to catch a sea turtle that had been swimming around the ship. Before the boy could get back aboard, the wind picked up and the ship sailed off, leaving the doomed young sailor clinging to the turtle. The ship and crew eventually reached the coast of Guatemala, and their descriptions of giant tortoises and marine iguanas are considered proof of a visit to the Galápagos Islands.

There was little more human intrusion into the Galápagos until the late 17th century, when buccaneers used the islands for a base. Some Spanish caravels had stopped at the islands in the meantime, but they found little food or fresh water. They did, however, name the islands Las Islas Encantadas (The Enchanted Islands), perhaps because the unpredictable currents, coupled with the fog that rolls in, often make the islands appear to be moving.

Flemish cartographer Abraham Ortelius, producer of the original modern atlas, was the first person to name the islands in honour of the giant land tortoises. The Galápagos appeared as "Insulae de los Galopegos" in his *Theatrum Orbis Terrarum* in 1570. In 1892, Ecuador officially renamed the islands Archipiélago de Colón (Columbus Archipelago) to honour the 400th anniversary of Christopher Columbus's discovery of America, but the name did not stick. Archipiélago de Colón is seldom used, except on Ecuadorian maps and documents; as one old-timer residing in the islands put it, "Galápagos isn't their name, it's only what they're called."

In the 1680s, the Galápagos Islands, because of their seclusion, became a strategic port for buccaneers. For the next 100 years, British pirates used the Galápagos as a clandestine base from which to harass and attack Spanish vessels that plied the coastal waters of South America. The pirates' visits triggered the dissolution of the delicate balance that existed between all flora and fauna on these lava-studded islands, a balance that had evolved over millennia. But strangely, it was goats, rather than humans, that would impose the earliest chaos on the Galápagos ecology.

After a particularly successful attack on three Spanish galleons off the coast of Peru, British Captain John Cook, aboard the *Bachelor's Delight*, went looking for the Galápagos Islands. According to William Cowley, one of Cook's officers, the *Bachelor's Delight* and the *Nicholas*, loaded with booty, "sailed away to the Westwards to see if wee could find those Islands called the Galipoloes, which made the Spaniards laugh at us, telling us that they were enchanted Islands and that there was never any but

Capitaino Porialto that had ever seen them but could not come near them to Anchor at them, and they were but Shadowes and no reall Islands." However, they did find the Galápagos Islands, where they cached some of their booty, which included a few goats.

In a remote archipelago such as the Galápagos, where animals and plants have adapted to the simplified island ecosystems in relative isolation, the introduction of a new species can be disastrous. Without natural enemies to keep their numbers in check, the goats flourished, depleting plant communities to the point that the tortoises' food supply began to disappear. To make matters worse, other animals such as rats and dogs also went ashore. In a single visit, the buccaneers ruined the ecological balance that had evolved over thousands of years.

If the Galápagos Islands lost their virginity to the buccaneers, they lost a great deal more to whalers and sealers. Between 1780 and 1860, commercial hunters harvested whales and fur seals from the rich Galápagos waters, sustaining themselves by stockpiling tortoises, to be consumed later as a source of fresh meat. The tortoise populations on accessible islands such as Española, Santa Fe, Marchena and Pinta suffered the most, as tens of thousands of these giant reptiles were taken from the islands and crammed into the dingy holds of ships.

In 1813, Captain Porter of the U.S. frigate *Essex* noted: "Here, wood is to be obtained, and land tortoises in great numbers, which are highly esteemed for their excellence and are remarkable for their size, weighing from three to four hundredweight each. Vessels on whaling voyages among these islands generally take on board from two to three hundred of these animals and stow them in the hold where, strange as it may appear, they have been known to live for a year without food or water and, when killed at the expiration of that time, found greatly improved in fatness and flavour." In a subsequent visit to the islands, Captain Porter wrote: "We began to lay in our stock of tortoises, the grand object for which every vessel anchors at the Galápagos Islands. Four boats were dispatched every morning for this purpose and returned at night, bringing with them from 20 to 30 each, averaging about 60 pounds. In four days, we had as many on board as would weigh about 14 tons, which was as much as we could conveniently stow." Researcher Ian Thornton, author of *Darwin's Islands*, found reference in one whaler's log to 15,000 tortoises taken between 1811 and 1844.

The smaller subspecies were preferred, for they could be carried more easily, and now, only 11 of 14 subspecies of Galápagos tortoise (*Geochelone elephantopus*) exist, some surviving solely through the assistance of programmes initiated by the Charles Darwin Research Station. When the whalers and sealers raided the northern island of Pinta, they were exceptionally efficient at rounding up the tortoises; however, they did miss one male tortoise there. Visitors today can see the last remaining tortoise, affectionately named Lonesome George, at the research station. The world will lose another irreplaceable subspecies when he dies.

Ecuador took possession of the islands in 1832, hoping to extract income from the various whaling operations that visited them. That year, Colonel Ignacio Hernandez established a small colony on Isla Floreana, made up mainly of political detainees who traded prison terms for deportation. They grew maize, sugar cane, sweet potatoes and fruit but, more important, introduced cattle, horses, pigs and donkeys to an island that could not afford to support new species. Within a few years, the animals had destroyed the island's tortoise population through competition for food, and the colonists were forced to rely on other islands for tortoise meat.

A number of other islands were colonized: San Cristóbal in 1869 by a tyrannical sugar and lichen merchant who was finally murdered by his slave labourers in 1904; Isabela in the 1890s, first by vagrants from the streets of Guayaquil and later by convicts; and Santa Cruz in the 1920s by a group of naïve Norwegians quite unprepared for its isolation and arid climate.

As we approached Devil's Crown, the *Normita*'s engine dropped to an idle, and my thoughts turned to diving. The captain anchored just outside the circle of rocks that marks the remains of an old volcanic cone near Isla Floreana, and Mario and I wasted no time in taking the Zodiac around to the northern side of the Crown, where we began to dive.

Beneath the surface, a strong current moved us eastward over a sandy seafloor peppered with huge boulders. Everywhere we looked, we saw schools of fish—thousands of finned creatures,

The Galápagos batfish (*Ogcocephalus darwini*) hops about using its pectoral and pelvic fins as legs. Batfish have a natural fishing lure on their underside that they wiggle to attract small fish within eating range.

Bluechin parrotfish (*Scarus ghobban*), like this one, use their hard teeth to snap off coral and rock. After grinding it down at the back of their throats, they extract the nutrients and expel the waste — up to 200 pounds a year — as sand.

like colourful dabs of paint dropped on the canvas of the sea.

Among the queen angelfish and grunts, I noticed several grazing green-and-red parrotfish. With mouth agape, a 16-inch parrotfish lunged at patches of coralline algae and just plain rock, eating pieces of the hard substrate. These crunchers of coral and rock have teeth that resemble two semicircles of smooth ceramic. A small "grinding mill" at the back of the throat crushes the coarse material into fine particles that move onward to the stomach. Nutrients are extracted, and the rest is passed into the water at the rate of more than 200 pounds of sand per year.

I spotted Mario stretched out on the sand motioning to me. Three feet in front of him lay a most peculiar fish, one not commonly seen: the Galápagos batfish. This fish is six to eight inches long and built somewhat like a Cessna airplane, although its "wings" taper more gently to the rear. The dark skin covering its back is offset nicely by its cherry-red "lips." The batfish avoids movement as much as possible, preferring to rest on sandy ground, perched on a set of "landing gear" located under its wings. It can actually walk with these "legs" but covers larger distances by swimming. I finished photographing the batfish and watched

A school of scalloped hammerhead sharks (*Sphyrna lewini*), which measure up to 16 feet, patrols the murky waters off Devil's Crown, while I try to keep out of sight.

A spiked sea star (*Nidoriella armata*) picks its way over a rocky ledge crowded with a marine community of tube corals, encrusting algae, sponges, ascidians, hydroids and sea urchins. The vitality of some areas held a continual fascination for me, and it was possible to spend long periods of time examining the organisms in just a few square feet of seafloor.

A sea star (*Linckia* sp), three feet
long from arm tip to arm tip,
crawls slowly across the seafloor.
Several of its tube feet can be seen
protruding from beneath some of
its arms.

as it prepared to fin away. It raised itself on an additional set of legs under its tail section, like a Hovercraft switching into high gear, and swam 20 feet before touching down with a perfect four-point landing.

Later that afternoon, we returned to the same location on the outer north side of the cone. The tide had changed, and the current pushed us westward until we cleared the western end of Devil's Crown. The bottom there stretches out in a monotonous expanse of sand, and I had almost decided to call off the dive when we happened upon what can only be described as a field of snakes standing upright like so many walking canes. Mario and I had stumbled upon a congregation of garden eels. The Galápagos garden eel (*Taenioconger klausewitzi*) was an undescribed species until 1983, long after the great naturalist William Beebe had given other members of these snakelike fish their common name of garden eels. These 15-to-20-inch-long eels dig burrows into the sand and stand straight above their holes to dine on passing plankton, their tiny mouths set at an oblique angle to facilitate catching their food. As I approached, they gradually lowered their serpentine bodies into their dens; as soon as I backed away, they would pop up, just out of camera range. Despite numerous attempts, I was unable to obtain clear photographs of them. That night, we anchored in the bay at Punta Cormorant at the northern tip of Isla Floreana, and I opted for a good night's sleep, instead of a night dive.

The mystique of the Galápagos Islands is best revealed during those magical pre-dawn moments when nighttime retreats against the advancing light of the rising sun. Out of darkness, ethereal shadows give way to solid landscapes; the quacks and wood-wind whistles of blue-footed and masked boobies resound off hill and wave; and the scent that is unmistakably Galápagos pervades the air.

Refreshed after a deep sleep, my spirit of discovery was rekindled by the dawn. I was soon bouncing along in the Zodiac as Mario steered us toward the northeastern edge of Devil's Crown where, he assured me, we would find hammerhead sharks. I admit to a long-standing obsession for these extraordinary creatures, and now, perhaps, I would get my fill.

Devil's Crown is shark-infested. In the basin formed by the outer rock walls of the sunken volcanic crater, however, few sharks venture, and tourists who snorkel there seldom sight them. But outside the rocky ring, it is a shark-watcher's dream. Drawn by the abundance of fish, local Galápagos and white-tip sharks

115

The uniformity and denseness of fish schools never ceased to amaze me. Feeling secure in such a crowd, these grunts (*Orthopristis* sp), evenly spaced and travelling at the same speed, swept by me fearlessly.

are quite often joined by larger offshore sharks, such as hammerheads and the occasional tiger, to feed on the grunts, snappers and parrotfish.

A hundred feet from shore, I rolled overboard and immediately sighted a shark so big that my arms would have been unable to encircle its abdomen. I slowed my descent and searched my surroundings for a rocky backdrop to use for protection, if necessary, but the seafloor was flat. The hammerhead was swimming 25 feet away, and by the time I had reached the bottom, at a depth of 35 feet, two more hammerheads had joined it. I stared, awestruck, at the largest sharks I had ever encountered. Objects appear magnified 25 percent underwater, but by using the size of the Zodiac as a reference, I estimated that the hammerheads ranged from 12 to 16 feet in length.

Unfortunately, the great hammerheads did not swim close enough for a clear photograph. The water was clouded by minuscule debris carried by the substantial current, and while I did photograph a couple of hammerheads to record the experience, I realized the pictures would be of poor quality. Even had this not been the case, however, I knew no picture could convey the humbling experience of coming face to face with an animal that could tear me to pieces.

Mario and I proceeded to the base of the northeastern wall of Devil's Crown, where tumbled rocks form tunnels, arches, overhangs and deep crevices. The current swept us westward, and we cruised through the passageways, careful to avoid being trapped in places too small for diver and tank. If not for the threat of decompression sickness, I could have spent the entire day underwater photographing the fish life and still would not have begun to complete recording all the species and colours and shapes. At times, I simply knelt on the seafloor while countless fish descended upon me in a whirling mass.

In a large corral formed by boulders, I took pictures of a school of grunts. I had to wave my hand in front of the camera periodically to force the fish away from the lens so that I could get them in focus. Sometimes, the grunts were so densely packed, I had trouble spotting an individual fish to photograph. Perhaps, I mused, this was the grunts' way of confusing large predators looking for a single fish upon which to prey. I ascended, leaving the fish milling about.

As I reached the top of the rocky pen, I stopped abruptly at the sight of one of the great mysteries of the sea. Swimming 30 feet away was a school of 12 to 14 great hammerhead sharks.

These were scalloped hammerheads (*Sphyrna lewini*), the most common of the three species of these bizarre sharks found in the Galápagos. Of all sharks, the hammerhead is most easily identified, bearing a mallet-shaped head with an eye at each end of the perpendicular stalk. Hammerheads frequently travel in small groups, and it is an awesome sight indeed to witness so many of those frightful-looking creatures at close range. They feed on fish, squid and crustaceans and have been identified in shark attacks on humans.

The school of hammerheads swam past slowly, seemingly unaware of my presence. Thinking that perhaps they had not seen me, I emerged from behind the rocks, and the sharks immediately turned 180 degrees. Because of the awkward position of its eyes, the hammerhead is forced to turn its head sideways to see with both eyes. As the school passed me from left to right, the sharks dipped their right eyes and raised their left in a coordinated primordial salute. I took one picture and then found my film was spent. I watched helplessly as the school disappeared.

Later that morning, we again dived the northeast face of Devil's Crown. We hoped to sight more hammerheads, but none appeared. Fish abounded, but the visibility had worsened as a result of the stronger current. After a half-hour dive, we moved on to Isla Champion, southeast of Devil's Crown.

We dropped anchor that afternoon on the lee side of Isla Champion. The wind was whipping the sea from the southeast, and the calm waters on the western side of Champion, facing Isla Floreana, offered the most sheltered dive site. Mindful of the amount of time we had already spent underwater that day, Mario and I contented ourselves with crisscrossing the upper 40 feet of the drop-off, where large coral formations shape the underwater seascape. The most prominent coral growth stood three to four feet high, forming a mound with layers fanning outward to a base six feet across. These corals belong to the genus *Pavona*, a coral found in most reef habitats and one of the few reef-building corals capable of surviving the cool waters of the Galápagos.

I sprawled at the base of a coral mound and observed a 14-inch-long sea cucumber making its way along the bottom. Resembling an oversized warty caterpillar, the sea cucumber moves slowly over the seafloor ingesting detritus. Enzymes digest the algae, and stomach acid partially dissolves calcium carbonates, leaving indigestible material to exit the anus (known as the cloaca to biologists) in a pencil-shaped trail. A loathsome-looking creature, it possesses a specialized cloaca, for unlike most marine animals

Vacuum cleaners of the seafloor, sea cucumbers (*Isostichopus fuscus*) move along the bottom ingesting detritus. After digesting algae and calcium carbonates, they leave the rest behind in a thin trail of waste.

that have gills located near head and mouth, the sea cucumber breathes through its anus.

I then spied several red squirrelfish hiding in fissures in the coral. Squirrelfish are nocturnal feeders that conceal themselves in caves and corals during the day. At sundown, as they emerge, they make a weird sound not unlike that of a duck quacking. Although many fish on the coral reef make noises, few can change pitch like the squirrelfish as it heads into an aggressive encounter or warns of danger. The underwater world can, at times, be anything but silent.

The next morning found the sky hung with ominous black clouds and the wind blowing forcefully from the southeast. It was the end of June, and the cold Antarctic current had pushed its way into the islands, causing unstable weather. I had decided to return to Canada after this swing through the south. I still had the northern marine province to explore, but it would have to wait until the new year when conditions would be more favourable for diving and photography. I had been in the Galápagos Islands for almost four months, and though I had taken thousands of pictures, I had not seen one of them developed.

Because of the rough seas, we scrapped plans to dive Isla Gardner farther to the southeast and chose the southern face of Isla Champion instead. It proved to be uninteresting at best for taking photographs: the only bright spot occurred near the surface, where encrusting sponges and a few hydroids and orange tunicates clung to the rocks. Mario and I returned to the *Normita*, frustrated that our diving was so unproductive.

Bonnie Burns and Jan Stepanoff, meanwhile, were searching for shells at every stop and were experiencing better luck. They had already discovered a couple of new species and a very rare *Conus* while diving at Devil's Crown and Punta Cormorant. It was an amazing feat, considering that there are more than 100,000 identified species of mollusks in the world (only the huge phylum Arthropoda, which includes insects, spiders and crabs, is larger).

The shells of mollusks comprise an unbelievable array of shapes and ornamentations. Not all the ocean's mollusks have shells — for example, octopuses and nudibranchs — but those that do have protective shells begin life as tiny larvae which are carried at the mercy of ocean currents, ensuring the dispersion of the species. Near the end of the larval stage, they drop to the seafloor, where they will advance to their adult forms if the substrate is suitable. It is during this stage that the beautifully patterned and intricately detailed shells are formed.

This sheet coral (*Pavona* sp) serves as a resting place for a couple of gobies (*Lythrypnus* sp). One of the few reef-building corals in the Galápagos, it grows to several feet across and makes an excellent refuge for fish.

As I turned over this horse conch (*Fascioloria princeps*) for a closer look, it began to retract its fleshy bright red foot. Once inside its armour, it is practically invulnerable.

Aboard the *Normita*, I had taken off my wet suit and was enjoying the warmth of snug dry clothes and hot tea when a yell from across the water caught my attention. Jan had found some sea horses, fish I had yet to see and was eager to photograph. Quickly, I tore off the cozy pants and sweatshirt, pulled on my cold, wet diving suit and within minutes was back in the water.

A pair of seven-inch-tall sea horses stood among a lonely stand of black coral, their tails coiled tightly around the stalks. After taking a few pictures, I reached down to coax them into a different position and was surprised by their cooperative nature. Rather than swimming away, they allowed me to pick them up, their rough skin-covered exoskeleton allowing a solid grip.

The first one I grasped, however, startled me by snapping its neck—a peculiar habit of the species—which sounded like a knuckle cracking. If it was a defensive measure, it worked, for I dropped the sea horse immediately, allowing it to swim away. It used its tiny fins like a hummingbird's wings to hover and then moved ahead by leaning forward like someone straining against

a driving rain; but it was slow, and I had no trouble catching the wayward creature.

After capturing a pair, I carried the sea horses carefully to the surface and deposited them in a bucket. We identified them as *Hippocampus ingens*, the only species of sea horse in Galápagos waters and the largest in existence. All 20 species of sea horse are true bony fish like cod or salmon, and they share the same order— Gasterosteiformes—as trumpetfish and cornetfish, those long, narrow fish with pronounced underbites. Yet the sea horse has one characteristic that it shares only with its closest relative, the pipefish: the usual sexual roles and breeding habits are reversed.

Following an elaborate courtship dance, the female sea horse transfers her eggs to the male's pouch, where they are brooded for about three or four weeks. When giving birth, the male goes through a series of convulsions, ejecting the young a few at a time through a hole at the top of the pouch. The newborn sea horse immediately swims to the surface and gulps air to fill its swim bladder, a remarkable organ which affords the sea horse almost

A small school of squirrelfish (*Myripristis leiognathos*) circles about the mouth of a cave, a favourite daytime retreat. Nocturnal feeders, squirrelfish emit a quacking noise, changing pitch if danger is present.

neutral buoyancy so that it can hover above the seafloor without expending much energy. The young then return to the depths to be raised to maturity by the male parent.

Later, Bonnie, Jan, Mario and I dived the protected waters inside Devil's Crown, where there is a large cavern with openings at both ends, its ceiling dotted yellow with anemone-like zoanthids. A school of squirrelfish was concealed in the shaded reaches, and sea lions swam in and out of the cave.

At the end of the afternoon, we took shelter in the cove at Punta Cormorant. The early evening typified the routine we had developed while at sea in the Galápagos Islands: we transferred the photography and diving equipment from the Zodiac to the *Normita* and hung the suits, fins, masks and regulators on ropes that stretched between guy wires and wooden posts. The noisy gas engine that drove the compressor was put into service, and for the next hour or two — depending on the number of tanks to be filled — it pumped clean, dry air into the scuba tanks. The compressor required periodic checks to drain the separator, remove a full cylinder and replace it with an empty one and to make sure that the coil cooling the air being pumped into the tanks did not overheat.

While the tanks filled, I worked on my camera equipment. The photographic paraphernalia essential for taking a camera underwater demands preventive maintenance to ensure smooth operation and to avoid a flooded camera or strobe. The bulky and expensive housing in which the camera is secured prevents access to the camera and lens when underwater. It must be in perfect working order before the dive begins, for there is no opportunity to make corrections while submerged.

Between dives, I simply changed film in the camera and performed a quick check of the main O-ring seal to see that it was free of dirt — even a piece of sand lodged in the O-ring could allow corrosive salt water to enter the housing and damage the camera. After a full day of diving, I followed a more thorough maintenance routine. On my bunk below deck, I unsnapped the latches that hold together the front and back halves of the housing, rewound the exposed roll of film in the camera and replaced it with a fresh one. I checked the mechanical levers, ensuring that they were functioning properly, and cleaned and greased the main O-ring that seals the join where the front of the housing meets the back. The port, an optically corrected piece of glass through which the lens "sees," was wiped clean with a soft cotton shirt, and the strobe cord was plugged into the bulkhouse connector

A seven-inch-long sea horse (*Hippocampus ingens*) hovers in front of sheet coral (*Pavona* sp) browsing for food. The only sea horse species in the Galápagos, it is the largest in the world, often growing to a foot in height.

to test the integrity of the connection. If the electrical junction was sound and the strobe fired upon releasing the shutter, I knew the unit was ready for the next dive. With four complete housing and camera units with me, the cleaning and reloading process took almost an hour, but it was time well spent. Having four cameras at my disposal meant that I could shoot more film during my limited time underwater and make fewer trips to the surface to reload.

The strobes I use are specially designed for underwater work. Their potent flash equals the coverage of a 20mm lens, and they generally store enough power to fire off six rolls of 36-exposure film. When they needed recharging, I started the small Honda generator and plugged in the chargers for several hours. With the compressor and the generator running, the *Normita* sounded like a factory ship.

In addition to the chores, evenings constituted a time for journal entries and discussions of the day's events, usually over dinner. Eduardo, who laboured in a galley that barely measured four by five feet, was a superb chef, imbuing the *Normita* with savoury odours. After diving and travelling, we were all famished and would take side trips to the galley to check on the progress and substance of the meal to come. Eduardo never disappointed us, and that evening, three days into our southern expedition, we dined on raw octopus marinated in lime juice, onions and spices; rice; grilled grouper; and deep-fried bananas. For dessert, I brought out some chocolate, and Jan had a jar of peanut butter he had brought with him from New York. We ended our meal with the Galápagos equivalent of peanut-butter cups.

Normally, after dinner, everyone would file below to lie on a bunk to read or to fill in a logbook before drifting off to sleep, for mornings came early. However, Jan, Mario and I postponed our trip below deck that night in order to explore the reef at the entrance to the cove. Mario stayed aboard the Zodiac, tracking Jan and me by the glow of our lights underwater. This dive marked Jan's initiation into the world of the night sea, and it pleased me to be the one to accompany him. Nothing exists topside to compare with the serenity of the sea at night or the exhilaration that it inspires. We explored the reef for three-quarters of an hour, peeking into holes where fish slept and nocturnal invertebrates busily carried out routines little changed from the behaviour of their ancestors. A juvenile poison-tipped sea urchin perched on a rock — its pure white needle-sharp spines forming a royal crown — caught my eye, and I finished two rolls of

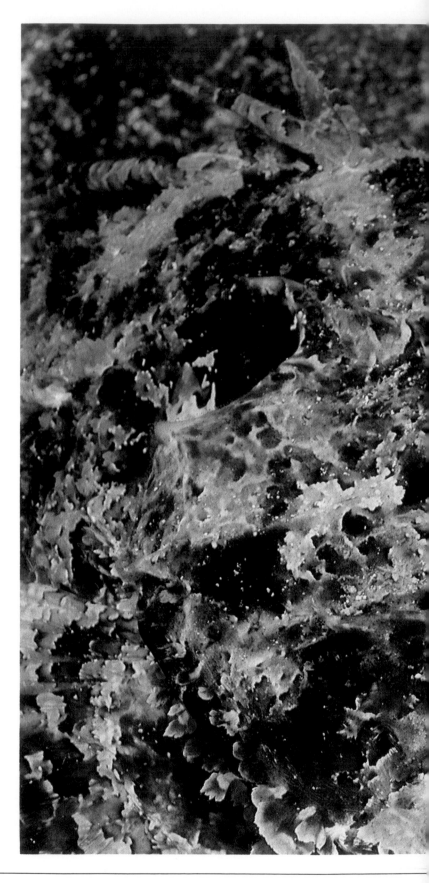

Made visible by two poison-tipped dorsal fins at the base of its head, the scorpionfish (*Scorpaena plumieri mystes*) seems a part of the seabed clutter. Mario and I caught this one for a scientist at the Darwin Research Station.

Once in a crevice, this octopus
(*Octopus* sp) altered its colour to
match the surroundings,
prompting a goby (*Lythrypnus* sp)
to rest on it. I could only see the
suckers on its tentacles and a
barely visible eye.

what I'd seen on the west coast of Isla Isabela) that indicated the Cromwell Current extended this far east, we were disappointed, for the barren sandy bottom offered little of interest.

We moved east again and explored the gradually sloping sea-bed near Isla Enderby, east-northeast of Isla Champion, where smooth holes scooped out of the rocky bottom gave the impression of Swiss cheese. Several octopuses occupied these dens, and a collection of black sea urchins made pincushions of the seascape. A large filefish crossed my path, its body a pleasing mosaic of blues and yellows, with the peculiar appearance of a fish swimming upside down.

We moored that night at Isla Champion. After a late supper, I loaded the bucket with our two sea horses into the Zodiac and motored to where Jan had found them. The stars shone fiercely that moonless night, and as I returned my two-day companions to the sea, I was able to follow their phosphorescent descent. For a brilliant instant, I was caught between the light of the sky and the glow of the sea.

A two-hour run down the east coast of Isla Floreana the following morning brought us to the north side of Isla Gardner (there are two Islas Gardners: one beside Isla Española to the east; and the other where we anchored near Isla Floreana). Massive boulders lay scattered on a sharply sloping bottom, looking as if they were about to cascade down the hill. In 25 feet of water, Mario halted his descent and excitedly beckoned to me. The cause of his agitation constituted a rare find indeed. Stationed at the mouth of its den lay a muppet-faced zebra moray eel (*Echidna zebra*). Alternating white and dark brown bands along its seersucker skin easily confirmed its identity. The first specimen of a zebra moray from the Galápagos had only recently been collected in the islands to the extreme north of the archipelago. In the far south, I was able to secure the first photographic record of this species in the islands. Mario had demonstrated his worth once again. During the rest of the dive, I lost myself in the forests of black corals that grew at depths of 70 to 100 feet.

At Isla Caldwell, later that day, Mario and I entered the water at the base of the steep cliffs on the northern side. Below the tide line, the rock face continues to plunge to depths unreachable by a scuba diver. A few crevices scar the smooth wall, and in these, invertebrates, lobsters, moray eels and fish compete for precious living space. We drifted eastward with the quickening current past stony protrusions and the largest single stand of Panamanian black coral I had seen, its main stalk almost two inches in diam-

One of my contributions to Galápagos subtidal research was the discovery of this zebra moray eel (*Echidna zebra*) off Isla Gardner. Although two of these muppet-faced characters had been found in the north, there had been no previous photographic record of them anywhere in the archipelago.

eter. Several times, I spotted sea turtles, hammerhead and Galápagos sharks and schools of sleek California yellowtails.

Clearing the eastern shore, Mario and I surfaced to an angry sea. We bobbed about in five-to-six-foot swells caused by a southeasterly sea running smack into the powerful current. We could not see Eduardo in the Zodiac anywhere. Had our air supply not been low, we could have dived beneath the waves and worked our way underwater in the direction of the *Normita*, but I had only 300 psi of air remaining, which would have been exhausted in minutes straining against the underwater current. On the surface, we gained little headway in the face of the tidal flow, and we both began to tire. It was fruitless to fight the current any longer, so I began kicking toward the island 75 feet away, with the intention of securing a foothold before the current carried us far out to sea. I had closed the gap considerably when the Zodiac appeared from around the north side of the island. Our struggle against the current had taken its toll, though, and Mario, normally quiet and congenial, tied into Eduardo for having lost sight of us. It was an understandable mishap, for it is difficult to follow a trail of bubbles when the water is rough, but Mario was angry enough to ignore such considerations and would not give Eduardo credit for having come looking for us when he did.

Rough sea conditions thwarted our attempt to spend the night at Las Cuevas Cove on Isla Floreana, so we returned to Isla Champion. At 4 o'clock the next morning, I went topside to spend a quiet moment before having to wake the captain. Suddenly, the water off the stern exploded in a flash of light. Two streaks of fluorescent green zigzagged below the surface as Galápagos sea lions rocketed through an ebony sea, exciting the tiny phytoplankton that shone with bioluminescence, leaving glowing tunnels in their wake.

While under way to Isla Santa Fe, a strong current slowed our advance, and a choppy sea slammed us broadside, tossing us to and fro. I downed two cups of tea in a vain attempt to drive off the cold of a miserable dark morning. Weather conditions change rapidly in the Galápagos Islands at that time of the year, though, and as we prepared to dive at the caves along the northeast shore of Isla Santa Fe, the sun's rays squeezed through every tiny crack in the clouds. We swam to the openings of the large caverns and explored the areas that dipped into the sea. Surprisingly, we found walls carpeted with sponges, ascidians, zoanthids and hydroids. Current action and the flow of nutrients must have been greater than I thought, for I had not expected such a diversity of benthic

creatures. Photographing this close to the surface comes at the expense of a torn wet suit, bloodied hands and few good pictures, because it is impossible to remain steady while the ocean rises and falls against the coast. Given an unusual subject, however, such as the colonies of sea squirts there, it is all worthwhile.

The bottom sloped gradually away from the coast of Isla Santa Fe, and I came upon a sea turtle sleeping beneath an overhang. It started and tried to drive past me for the open sea, but I grabbed its shell behind its neck and hitched a ride. The sea turtle's carapace was barely three feet in diameter, but the strong flippers pumped with such force that I had to hang on tightly to avoid being thrown. Not wanting to lose track of the camera gear I had put down before latching on to the turtle and not knowing where we were headed, I finally let go and swam back to shore.

We spent that afternoon and evening in a picturesque cove on the northeast side of Isla Santa Fe, and I dived in the quiet, shallow waters of the bay photographing playful sea lions. The next morning, we did a deep 110-foot dive on the north shore of Santa Fe, and knowing this would probably be my last dive for several months to come, I lingered below with the coral and fish for as long as possible.

On the way back to Puerto Ayora, I packed my equipment, brought my journal up to date and basked under the sun in my favourite resting spot at the bow of the *Normita*. Canada seemed far, far away.

A Pacific green sea turtle (*Chelonia mydas agassizii*) makes its way over a reef. Despite their heavy carapace and large size, the turtles are powerful swimmers that can race through the water with surprising speed.

A large moray eel (*Lycodontis castaneus*) warns me away with a fierce display as I come within inches of its razor-sharp teeth.

The Humboldt Factor

Probing the murky depths of the northern islands

In less than two hours, Mario and I were suiting up to dive at the northeast edge of the largest rock at Rocas Gordon. I had not dived since my last excursion at Isla Santa Fe seven months before, and as I hovered a few minutes in the cool water, dozens of 50-pound amberjacks swam about me, and once again, I felt the exhilaration of diving in the Galápagos Islands. I was among old friends.

Later that afternoon, we moored at the neighbouring Islas Plazas, and I snorkeled in the sheltered channel between the two islands, photographing sea lions. A substantial rookery exists on the northern shore of Isla Plaza Sur, which provides a wealth of most cooperative subjects. There is no modesty among the sea lions of the Galápagos Islands, and they lined up in front of the camera, jostling for position to squeeze into the frame.

At 2 o'clock the next morning, beneath a starry sky, we left Islas Plazas for Isla Genovesa, 70 miles to the north. Fiddi had said the trip would take eight hours, but the captain assured us that the *Orca* could cover the distance in six. By 8 a.m., we had not yet sighted land, and the captain expressed his fear that we had drifted westward with the current. Mike, who had charted our course, disagreed and, through quiet diplomacy, convinced the captain to maintain our heading. From the upper deck of the *Orca*, I scanned the horizon, my eyes straining for a glimpse of land. As the minutes ticked away, I found myself wondering just where we were or, for that matter, where we would end up.

If the captain were justified in his concern that the prevailing current had carried us westward, then the much larger Isla Marchena would come into sight at some point. But if he had miscalculated our direction and we skirted Isla Genovesa on the eastern side, we could steam northward for a long time before the captain would become convinced of his error. With no radar and not even a sextant on board to fix a sight, a course correction was impossible, because we did not know our true position. To avoid getting hopelessly lost, we would have had to turn about and head for the central islands until we encountered a familiar landmark to give us our bearings.

In the morning mist, Genovesa is impossible to discern on the horizon from far away because it is flat, standing no more than 250 feet above sea level. At 9 a.m., it was still not in sight, but I was pleased to see masked boobies flying overhead, a sure indication that land was within reach. A half-hour later, the tabletop island of Genovesa emerged from the haze, and everyone on board heaved a sigh of relief. We dropped anchor at 10

A few tunicates manage to force their reddish orange siphons through a blanket of buttercup-sized zoanthid anemones smothering the seafloor.

Although their playful nature
would have made them easy
hunting for the sealers of the 19th
century, the sea lions (*Zalophus
californianus wollebaeki*) of the
Galápagos were considered of no
commercial fur value.

Rich supplies of food ensure a
wonderland of benthic life. Tube
corals (*Tubastraea* sp), sponges
and zoanthid anemones crowd
together here in an elegantly
textured underwater tapestry.

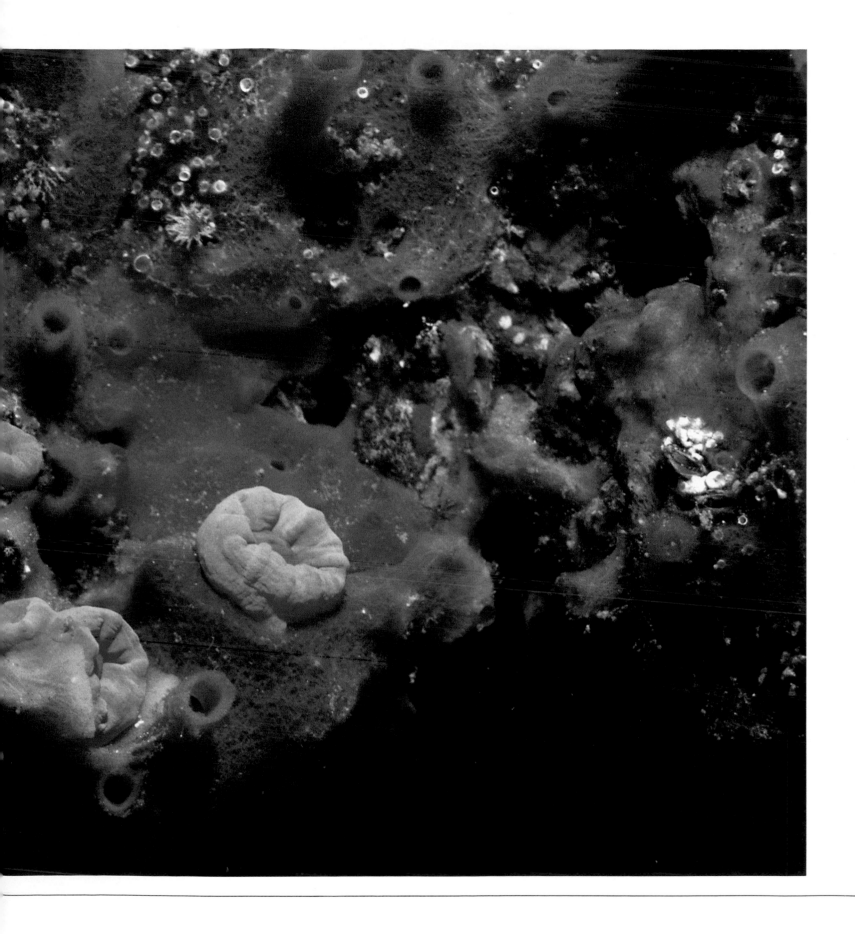

A pair of masked boobies (*Sula dactylatra*), their huge wings tucked in, rest on shore between feeding flights. Fascinating hunters, they spot their prey from high above the sea and rocket straight into the water to grab it.

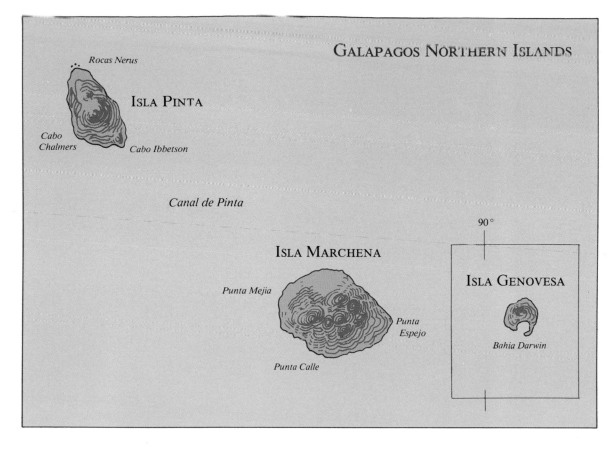

Rocas Nerus

ISLA PINTA

Cabo Chalmers

Cabo Ibbetson

Canal de Pinta

90°

ISLA MARCHENA

Punta Mejia

ISLA GENOVESA

Punta Espejo

Bahia Darwin

Punta Calle

o'clock in Bahia Darwin (a partially eroded volcanic crater that takes a giant bite out of the south side of Genovesa), confirming Fiddi's prediction of an eight-hour run from Islas Plazas.

Mike, Mario and I took the Zodiac along the eastern face of the bay where steep walls drop to the sea, and we searched for signs of an interesting dive site. But it was a discouraging hunt in the murky depths. The waters of Isla Genovesa seemed to be living up to their reputation for poor visibility; at one point, I slipped overboard and proved that my concerns were well founded. Sediment and plankton obscured the sea wherever I looked, and visibility was 10 to 20 feet at best. Diving there would have been a wasted effort, so we returned to the *Orca.*

Mario and I were disappointed, as we had both looked forward to diving these unusual waters for some time. While the islands of Pinta, Marchena and Genovesa resemble those of the central region of the Galápagos, there are distinct differences underwater, mainly due to the influence of northern tropical waters mixing with the cool waters of the Humboldt Current. There are more species of tropical fish, and the reefs of Bahia Darwin in particular are known for their ringtail tangs (*Acanthurus xanthopterus*), a species of Indo-Pacific surgeonfish seldom found in the central, southern or western marine provinces.

After changing out of our wet suits, all of us except the captain went ashore at the white coral beach on the west side of the bay. Behind the beach, great frigate birds were nesting in the green saltbushes, and as if in recompense to us for poor diving conditions, several males searching for mates inflated their beautiful scarlet throat patches. At least, I thought, the world topside would provide us with some distractions.

Separating the beach from the south coast of the island is a 15-foot-high wall of lava, a series of tide pools at its base filled by seawater that percolates through the lava via underground channels. The equatorial sun warms the water in these pools quickly, making them wonderful swimming holes. While Mike and Chelsea waded in, Mario and I hiked inland along an uphill corridor that brought us to the top of the lava ridge. We then walked south to the coast, where a cliff drops straight to the sea.

On our way back to the beach, I was startled to spot two people walking down from the higher regions; visitors seldom travel to Isla Genovesa, and ours was the only boat anchored in Bahia Darwin. After the couple had introduced themselves, however, I understood why I had not seen their camp. The park service requests that all scientists and photographers working in the vicinity of tourist sites make themselves as inconspicuous as possible, and they had secreted their tent well inland. This rule ensures that tourists restricted to footpaths will not have their view of nature ruined by signs of civilization and also, for the scientists' sake, will not be drawn to the campsites with endless questions. These were American biologists who had been on the

A small colony of orange tube corals (*Tubastraea* sp) rides along atop a blunt-spined sea urchin (*Eucidaris thouarsii*), certainly an odd attachment compared with its usual seabed locations.

island since before Christmas to study the breeding habits of one of the four species of Darwin finches found there. The finches had delayed breeding because of the prolonged dry conditions, and the biologists were patiently waiting for rain.

After a brief visit, we piled into the Zodiac, and after dropping off the others at the *Orca*, Mario and I headed for the east side of Bahia Darwin, where a series of natural steps (called Prince Philip's Stairs after the Duke of Edinburgh had visited the island) leads up the face of the bluff to the plateau. From there, a path wends through a small forest of aromatic Palo Santo trees where red-footed boobies like to nest. The largest colony of this species of booby in the Galápagos archipelago exists on Isla Genovesa, where the population is estimated to be 140,000 pairs. The forest opens onto a broad, flat clearing, home to thousands of masked boobies. Their crude nests of rocks and shells litter the ground, and often, we had to leave the path briefly to bypass them. In some nests, awkward balls of pure white fluff stuck close to their parents.

The sheer number of boobies on Isla Genovesa alone indicates the richness of the waters surrounding the Galápagos Islands, since boobies depend entirely on fish and squid collected from the sea for their diet. The amount of fish required to feed the booby populations of the various islands must be astronomical.

We returned to the *Orca* and spent the night anchored in Bahia Darwin. I climbed into my bunk early, as I wanted a fresh start the next morning, hoping that our luck would improve on the island of Marchena, 30 miles to the west. When we left at 4 a.m., the sea was running out of the southeast, and the wind had freshened, adding a fair chop to the swells as we made our way toward Punta Espejo at the eastern end of the island. We were looking for two small rocks that jut out of the sea just south of the point, because they are noted for their teeming fish life, in general, and hammerhead sharks, in particular.

When we arrived at Isla Marchena 3½ hours later, Mario and I made our first dive. Groping along the gradually sloping bottom, we could make out the shadowy figures of thousands of fish darting around the lava outcroppings scattered over the seafloor. I even had several fleeting glances of hammerheads, but the visibility was only slightly better than at Isla Genovesa, and photography was out of the question.

Unlike the American biologists, I could not afford to wait a couple of months to conduct my study. The business of chartering boats and crew was expensive, and I was quickly running

As soft as cotton to touch, this
four-inch-square swatch of
colonial sea squirts clings to a reef.
At birth, the sea squirt is a free-
swimming larva with vertebrae but
soon gives up its mobility to
become a nondescript sac.

out of money. I had counted on good luck for my entire Galápagos exploration but had run out of it a few weeks too soon, prevented from finishing my work by millions upon millions of tiny bits of oceanic junk suspended in the water. Even after years of working on and in unpredictable ocean environments, I could not easily resign myself to the delays and disappointments inherent in nature.

In quiet desperation, we motored around to the calmer northern shore of Marchena in the hope that Punta Espejo was an isolated case, murky because the currents and swells had churned up sediment. But closer to shore, the water proved to be just as turbid, confirming my fear that the condition was not localized. It was probable that an undersea current had carried nutrients to the surface, providing phytoplankton with the food stock it needed to bloom into the billions of tiny plants which were obscuring the sea.

Whatever the cause, it was futile to remain in the north. The system responsible for reducing visibility was so extensive that

it could have lasted for weeks. Isla Pinta was 35 miles to the northwest, with Isla Wolf another 60 miles beyond it and Isla Darwin yet an additional 20 miles away. I briefly toyed with the idea of heading for Wolf or Darwin, for their tropical waters (too far north to be affected by the cool waters of the Humboldt Current) support such west Pacific fish as the redtail triggerfish (*Xanthichthys mento*) and open-ocean fish like jacks, mackerel and sharks. Stories abound of some unknown species, unnamed and uncollected, but the islands of Wolf and Darwin are so isolated that one just doesn't decide on short notice to sail in their direction. Besides, if the captain had had doubts about our position en route to the much closer island of Genovesa, I had little confidence in his ability to find the extreme northern islands of the Galápagos. I felt it would be more fruitful to spend the rest of my charter documenting other regions of the archipelago where clearer waters would likely be found. There were many areas south of the equator in the central marine province that I had not yet dived and still others that I had visited only briefly.

Made fearless by the islands' sanctuary status, Galápagos penguins (*Spheniscus mendiculus*) parade past a sleeping sea lion (*Zalophus californianus wollebaeki*). Until recently, the national park did not protect ocean environments, allowing them to deteriorate while the islands were rehabilitated.

A red cluster of social ascidians
crowds around a colonial sea
squirt. Their lives consist of
clinging to rocks, sucking in water
through one spout and, after
extracting suspended nutrients,
expelling it through another.

The trumpetlike pedicellariae and spines of a short-spined sea urchin (*Toxotneustes roseus*) provide a colourful but toxic first line of defence. The urchin sports a bottom-side mouth that it uses to scrape algae from rocks.

I directed the captain to set a course toward Isla Cousins, off the east coast of Santiago in the central marine province. The northern marine province is the least studied within the Galápagos Islands, and it seemed I would not be adding any information to the scientific literature on this excursion.

An hour south of Isla Marchena, the colour of the sea changed abruptly from green to blue. I stood at the stern of the *Orca*, and stretching eastward for as far as I could see was a distinct line delineating the boundary of two oceanic systems. The clearer water was tantalizingly close to where I wished to dive and photograph, but it might as well have been on the opposite side of the globe.

When we arrived at Isla Cousins that afternoon, Mario, Mike and I dived the inside face where the wall drops suddenly from the surface to 55 feet. A variety of benthic life clung to this wall, and I photographed the smaller forms of marine life extensively. At one point, I happened upon an eight-inch-square patch of colonial sea squirts. Dozens of tiny sacs, each about the size of a marble, painted the lava substrate a splendid orange. In appearance, the sea squirt, or ascidian, is much like the sponge, the lowliest of all multicelled animals. Like sponges, sea squirts depend on the ocean currents to bring food within reach, and they thrive in similar habitats; but looks can be deceiving, and in truth, sea squirts are more closely related to man than to the sponge.

Sea squirts belong to the phylum Chordata, which includes such members as whales, dogs and man. At birth, the sea squirt is a free-swimming larva that resembles a tadpole, and with the anatomy of a tiny vertebrate, it appears to be headed for a life of higher calling. But instead, the larva attaches its head to a rock and develops into a nondescript sac, eventually forming two spouts that it uses alternately to draw in and expel seawater. Any food that is suspended in the incoming seawater is trapped in the gut.

I moved on from the sea squirts and spent the rest of my time easing along the wall, stopping at leisure to take pictures of corals and sponges and the tiny fish that conceal themselves among these invertebrates. It is often the smaller life forms of the sea that provide the most interesting study, as evidenced by the strange sea squirts, and I became so intent on taking pictures that I was caught off guard when I checked my pressure gauge and found my air supply all but exhausted. We ascended and retired to the *Orca*.

That evening, we moored in Bahia Sullivan, between Isla Bartolomé and Isla Santiago. After supper, Mike and I dived a reef at the south end of the strait that Mike had previously investigated in daylight. We drifted through a black ocean to the seafloor and began to search the crevices and overhangs where fish tuck themselves away for the night. In one rocky hollow, I found an iridescent green parrotfish that became so mesmerized by my light that I could reach out and gently stroke its side. During the day, I would have been lucky to get within 10 feet of the same fish. An hour into the dive, my light dimmed and finally went out, forcing me to surface. On my ascent, I pushed a stream of phosphorescence before me as thousands of dinoflagellates bounced off my camera housing, emitting pulses of light.

As we motored south through the narrow passage between Sombrero Chino and Isla Santiago on the fourth day of our trip, Mike spotted penguins on the shore. On a ridge jutting out from Isla Santiago, five of them stood like dumpy little neckless statues, quite unconcerned by our approach in the Zodiac. I shot pictures of them topside, then slipped into the water, and after a long time, three of them leapt feet first into the water. They flapped about, using their wings to propel themselves at surprising speeds, and I could see how well equipped they were for capturing small fish, their staple food.

I climbed back into the Zodiac, and Mario steered across the channel to where a dozen sea lions lay fast asleep along the

At their rookery on Islas Beagles, Galápagos sea lions (*Zalophus californianus wollebaeki*) languish on a sandy beach. Such sea-level lounging is temporary, however, for incoming tides ultimately force them to higher ground.

idyllic beach on Sombrero Chino, their dark brown fur a stark contrast to the white sand. At both ends of the beach, *Sesuvium* plants were thriving close to the lava rocks, their brilliant red succulent leaves adding a welcome brush of colour to an otherwise drab landscape.

I wished to spend time probing the rocky shoreline of outer south James Bay on the west coast of Isla Santiago, around the area of the fur seal grottoes, so after dropping anchor in the bay later that afternoon, Mario and I took an extended walk along the coast. The strip between arid land and ocean upon which we strolled was the domain of hundreds of species of animals and plants. Those living close to the water's edge, such as barnacles, require frequent submersion in the sea, and as the tides ebb and flow, their stretches of shoreline are alternately exposed and inundated. The barnacle is able to withstand periods underwater and above, snaring food while submerged by sweeping with its fine hairy net through the tidal waters. To avoid drying out during low tide, it closes a series of plates at the opening of its shell, thereby preserving moisture against the desiccating effect of the sun.

One of the primary foods that support seashore life is algae, the plants of the sea. When Mario and I walked along the coast, the tide had just receded, and the verdant green algae that covered the rocks were still moist. Spread over the coast like a finely woven mat, the algae appeared to change colour from green to black as the sun angled toward the horizon. Marine iguanas worked the rocks close to the sea, heads turned sideways against the ground to graze on the luxuriant sea lettuce. Sally Light-foot crabs hustled over the carpet of algae, pausing now and then to pick at detrital foods. Oystercatchers stalked the pools, spearing the soft fleshy meat of any mollusk caught with its shell slightly ajar. Lava herons stood motionless beside a pool until their slender pointed beaks and long necks suddenly darted into the water, returning occasionally with a tiny writhing fish as a reward for their efforts. The entire coastline was alive with the business of survival.

At one point, we stopped beside a tide pool barely three feet in diameter to watch an interesting little drama. The star performance was staged not in the tide pool but at its periphery, where two large male Sally Light-foot crabs were attempting to copulate with a single female poised in a small hollow. One male would approach and mount from behind, literally entangling the female in legs and claws. Then, from over a ridge, the other

148

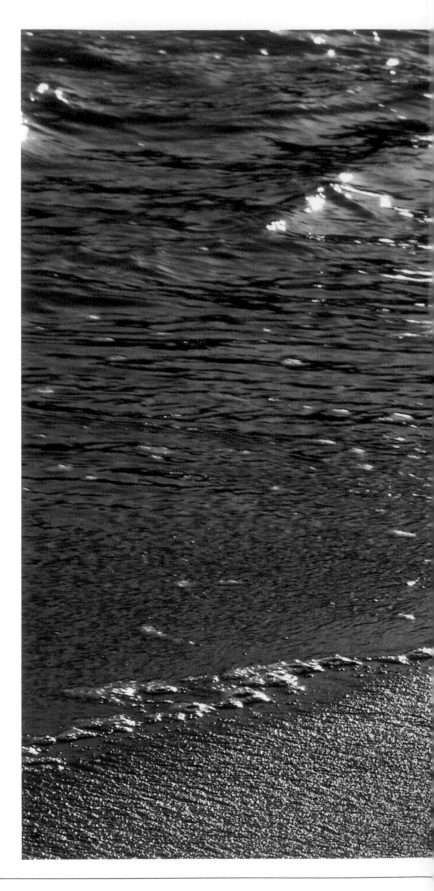

A beachcombing Sally Light-foot crab (*Grapsus grapsus*) skitters back and forth with the flow of the sea in search of food. The crabs feed on practically anything, a trait that keeps the shoreline free of animal debris.

meyer, for example, believes that you remain uninitiated into the archipelago until a frigate bird has deposited a dropping on you. I did not have to wait long for my own initiation, making the bird's acquaintance one afternoon aboard the *Bucanero* on my first journey to the islands. Photographing frigate birds as they effortlessly rode the air currents high above the boat, I had stopped to change film in my camera when one of them took aim and dropped a white bomb on the fragile shutter curtain inside the camera. I viewed that as an auspicious start and spent several hours delicately cleaning up the mess.

The next morning, we dived the eastern point of Isla Rábida to a depth of 60 feet, accompanied the whole time by a rather curious sea turtle. Before diving the Galápagos Islands, I had never seen a turtle underwater, and despite many sightings during my stay, I still loved to watch them swim. Broad flippers poke out from a rotund fortress of a shell, looking more like afterthoughts than parts of the original design. Yet awkward as a sea turtle appears when stroking the water simultaneously with all four flippers, it can move at considerable speeds.

Later that afternoon, Mario and I explored Caleta Tortuga Negra, the massive mangrove lagoon on northern Isla Santa Cruz. The sea turtle mating season was in full swing, and we observed many pairs performing their ritual in the tranquillity of an inlet. A male would climb upon a female's back, and together, they would paddle around the lagoon, surfacing periodically and breaking the silence with loud gasps for air. One pair clung together for more than half an hour before disappearing from sight beneath the surface. In some ways, I felt as if I were intruding on a prehistoric rite.

We spent the night moored off the lagoon and the following morning motored back around Isla Santa Cruz to Puerto Ayora. It was time for my return to Canada.

After a full day's work, I relaxed on the patio at the Hotel Solymar, sipping a cool drink of juice and contemplating my brief and less-than-successful excursion to the northern and central islands. At a table nearby, four tourists who had just returned from a week's charter around the central islands were recounting their adventures. Words such as "tremendous" and "unbelievable" punctuated their speech as they described the wonders they had witnessed: the giant tortoises and marine iguanas they could not have seen anywhere else in the world.

What these tourists did not seem to realize, despite their enthusiasm for the wildlife, was that in the 300 years since the

male would dash to the pair and challenge its opponent, forcing the occupied male to loosen its grip in defence. Both males would scramble briefly out of sight, until one of them dared approach the female again. I watched the battle for at least 10 minutes, but neither male seemed to make much headway, and as I walked back to the *Orca*, I wondered how Sally Light-foots could be so abundant on the coast when their mating seemed so problematic.

Overhead, a frigate bird, "vulture of the sea," harassed a masked booby, trying to upend it in flight by grabbing its tail or wing in an effort to force the booby to drop whatever food it was carrying. Frigate birds are most successful at this ploy, and when the booby regurgitates its food, the frigate bird can swoop down and snatch it out of the air. With a wingspan of eight feet and a body weight of a mere two to three pounds — the greatest wingspan-to-body-weight ratio of any bird in the world — frigate birds are one of the marvels of natural aviation.

A folklore has evolved among some inhabitants of the Galápagos Islands about the omnipresent frigate bird. Gus Anger-

After browsing leisurely on algae 15 feet below the surface, a marine iguana (*Amblyrhynchus cristatus*) comes up for air. While its claws are not well suited to swimming, they provide an excellent grip on the seafloor.

arrival of man, the natural world of the Galápagos has been turned upside down. If the islands' three to five million years of evolution were compressed into a 24-hour day, it would have taken us less than eight seconds to bring about what may be irreversible change. For the most part, this assault has now been halted. The declaration of national park status for the islands in 1959 and the institution of the Galápagos National Park Service in 1968 ensure not only the control of the flow of tourists but also, and more important, the restriction of access to ecologically sensitive islands and the implementation of management programmes designed to save those species in danger of extinction. Park regulations prohibit the hunting and collecting of the terrestrial life for souvenirs, and the new rules are enforced by a complement of guides and naturalists. If park personnel are as successful in their plans to exterminate feral animals such as dogs, pigs and goats, the creatures of the Galápagos Islands have a sound future.

The same prognosis, however, could not be made for the ma-

rine community: as terrestrial animals and plants were pulling themselves back from extinction, the subtidal world of the Galápagos was deteriorating.

At present, the ocean life surrounding these enchanted islands is ecologically sound. True, the results of overfishing have already forced local fishermen farther and farther from port in search of their catch; the lobster population has dwindled; black corals have been harvested at an alarming rate; and pollution from untreated sewage, diesel-fuel spills and leaking bilge oil has decimated oyster beds and threatened marine life near Puerto Ayora. But the point of no return has yet to be reached, and if all the harvesting is regulated to a level that the marine environment could safely tolerate and if pollution is reduced, there is little doubt the community could rebound.

The worst threat to the marine ecology stemmed from the local inhabitants who fished and harvested in response to the dictates of the market. On the table in front of the foursome of tourists at the Hotel Solymar stood a carved figurine of a Galápagos sea

A Pacific green sea turtle
(*Chelonia mydas agassizii*) bolts
from a cave, bound for the open
sea. Although its carapace was
only about three feet in diameter, I
grabbed onto it and hitched a ride,
amazed at the turtle's strength.

Young wrasses (*Bodianus diplotaenia*) swim about a stand of Galápagos black coral (*Antipathes galapagensis*). Too soft for carving, this coral remains healthy, but harder corals have been devastated by the souvenir trade.

lion, undoubtedly purchased from a local artisan. It was about three inches high, and judging by its silky ebony appearance, it had been shaped from a piece of black coral. Making some quick calculations, I guessed that if one-quarter of the 15,000 people who annually visit the Galápagos Islands purchase a single crafted piece of coral three inches long, then about 940 feet of black coral must be lost each year. If each coral tree yielded three feet of usable coral—a large tree indeed!—a minimum of 313 coral bushes would have to be cut down. No environment the size of the Galápagos could withstand such intensive, uncontrolled coral harvesting.

And, I asked myself, what will happen once the coral is gone? What other animals will the locals turn to in their quest for tourists' dollars? I recalled the grotesque stare of a bloated Caribbean pufferfish that had been made into a lamp. I had seen it a few years before in the window of a souvenir store in the French West Indies. Hard corals had long been depleted in the Caribbean, and the locals were capturing pufferfish and inflating and varnishing them to sell to tourists. With a light bulb wired inside, they became hideous mementos of a winter's stay in paradise. The Galápagos has pufferfish too, and I shuddered as I considered the souvenir-stand possibilities of one of the world's rarest marine environments.

The threat to the subtidal plants and animals of the Galápagos Islands has come not only from the locals, however. Each year, more scuba divers explore the vast uncharted waters, and many surface with more than just photographs and memories. Although I would estimate that less than 1 percent of the tourists who visit the archipelago scuba dive, the numbers have been increasing. Judy and Fiddi Angermeyer have had to purchase two air compressors to meet the demand of diving charters.

Lights began to flicker on along the shore of Puerto Ayora, and as I sat in the twilight, I felt a sense of accomplishment tinged with sadness. During my travels through the archipelago, I had seen a showcase of spectacular marine creatures, one-quarter of which occur nowhere else on this planet, but I was not confident that they were going to survive indefinitely. To me, the need for protection was indisputable, and the means of effecting it, through the existing park service, were already in place. The salvation of the Galápagos marine community lay tantalizingly close at hand, but that night, as I eased away from the table nodding good night to the group of chattering tourists, I was not convinced that anything would be done. The government had the oppor-

tunity in 1959 but had decided to limit the park service's control to the land, citing insufficient documentation of the subtidal environment to warrant park status. Ironically, as the value of the marine environment was confirmed over the years, the rate of its destruction increased.

A year and a half after brooding on the patio of the Hotel Solymar over the plight of the Galápagos subtidal world, I was delighted to learn that Léon Febres Cordero, Ecuador's president, had declared the waters of the Galápagos Islands a marine reserve. As of May 13, 1986, all inshore waters and all waters extending 15 miles off the outer coast of the islands were to be incorporated into the national park. After visiting the islands and the biologists who work there, Cordero became convinced that the underwater world of the Galápagos might prove of even more value scientifically than the islands.

While it would be premature to suggest that reserve status will bring funding for scientific assessments of the subtidal zone—research that would both establish the ocean environment's importance and catalogue its inhabitants—it will at least prevent further deterioration of sea life and give nature a chance to reestablish its rhythms and patterns.

This is the first step in the conservation of one of the planet's most exotic and magical environments. I rest easier knowing that my photographs will serve as an introduction to an exciting underwater kingdom rather than an incomplete record of a lost world.

The sun sets behind Pinnacle Rock on Isla Bartolomé. Now that there is legislation to protect subtidal Galápagos, I join with the other environmentalists who are hopeful that the fragile balance of the sea will be restored.

Index